D1267594

Jewels of Guidance

Advice from the Prophet Mohammad (pbuh)

Available from:
http://IslamicBookstore.com
+1 410-744-7393 Maryland, USA

Compiled by

Hamzah Muhammad Salih Ajjaj

مكتبة دار التقوى
DAR AL TAQWA LTD

New translation from the Arabic by
Muhammad Isa Waley

Third Edition. 1996

ISBN 1 870582 00 4

Translated by Muhammed Isa Waley

Published by:
Dar Al Taqwa Ltd.
7A Melcombe Street
Baker Street
London
NW1 6AE

Printed in Great Britain By:
DELUXE PRINTERS
245A Acton Lane, Park Royal
London NW10 7NR

Contents

Introduction

Next to the Glorious Qur'ān, the *Sunnah* or words and actions of the Prophet Muhammad (peace and blessings upon him), as reported by his Companions, constitute the most important source of Islamic knowledge. The collection of these reports or Traditions *(Ḥadīths,* Arabic plural *Aḥādīth)* began during the lifetime of the Prophet. Muhammad (*ṣ*) urged Muslims to acquire knowledge and transmit it to others – above all, knowledge concerning the Qur'ān and the Prophetic *Sunnah* as related in the Traditions.

Many Companions of the Prophet (*ṣ*) observed keenly all that they saw him do, and learned by heart whatever they heard him say. Some wrote down these reports and collected them in books (*ṣaḥīfahs,* Arabic plural *ṣuḥuf*) which were passed on to later generations; others taught them orally.

For Muslims, the Prophet represents the perfect human individual, whose ways should ideally be followed as closely as possible. His practices and instructions regarding every aspect of earthly existence should form the basis of every Muslim's daily life.

The authority of the Prophet Muhammad (*ṣ*) was not restricted to matters of legislation and religious observance. As a "Mercy to the Worlds", his eternal message also includes knowledge needed to help all mankind in solving spiritual and moral problems.

This fact is amply borne out in many of the *Ḥādīths* in this collection. They include prayers (*du'ā*'s, Arabic plural *ad'iyah*) used by the Prophet (*ṣ*) which may help the Believer to draw closer to Allah by following his example. "Verily in the Messenger of Allah you have an excellent example" (Qur'ān, *Sūrah* 33, verse 21).

Abbreviations used in this book: ṣ = *ṣallā 'Llāhu 'alayhi wa sallam* (may Allah give him blessings and peace). r = *raḍiya 'Llāhu 'anhu/'anhā/'anhumā* (may Allah be pleased with him/her/them both).

Chapter 1

The excellence of the words *"Lā ilāha illā 'Llāh* (There is no god but Allah)"

Abū Hurayrah (*r*) said: "I asked the Prophet (*ṣ*): 'O Messenger of Allah, who will be happiest with your intercession on the Day of Resurrection?' He said: 'I expected, Abū Hurayrah, that no one would beat you to this question, seeing your keen interest in *Ḥadīth*. Those who will be happiest with my intercession on the Day of Resurrection will be those who say There is no god but Allah sincerely, from their very heart and soul'".
(Related by al-Bukhārī)

It was reported by 'Ubādah ibn aṣ-Ṣāmit (*r*) that the Prophet (*ṣ*) said: "Whoever bears witness that there is no god but Allah, that He has no associates, that Muhammad is His servant and Messenger, that Jesus is His Servant, His Messenger, His Word which He passed unto Mary, and a Spirit from Him, that Paradise is real, and that Hell-Fire is real, Allah will admit him into Paradise, no matter what his deeds were".
(Related by al-Bukhārī, Muslim, and at-Tirmidhī)

Furthermore, the Prophet (*ṣ*) is reported to have said: "Whoever bears witness that there is no god but Allah and that Muhammad is His Messenger, Allah will forbid Hell-Fire to touch him".
(Related by Muslim)

Chapter 2

Tawḥīd (Divine Unity)

It is reported that Ibn 'Abbās (*r*) said: "I was once walking close behind the Prophet (*ṣ*), when he said: 'My boy, I am going to teach you a few words. Be mindful of Allah and He will be mindful of you; be mindful of Allah and you will find Him with you; if you ask, ask of Allah; if you seek help, seek it of Allah; know that if the whole Community (*Ummah*) joined hands so as to benefit you with something, they would not benefit you except with something that Allah had already written for you; and that if they joined hands to harm you with something, they would only harm you with something that Allah had already written for you. The pens have already been lifted away, and the pages have dried [from the ink with which the Decrees of Allah's Providence are written]'".
(Related by at-Tirmidhī)

In a different version of this *Ḥadīth*, the Prophet (*ṣ*) said: "Be mindful of Allah and you will find Him before you; make yourself known to Allah in your times of prosperity and He will recognize you in your times of hardship. Know, too, that what missed you could not have befallen you, and what befell you could not have missed you. Success goes hand in hand with perseverance; pleasure goes hand in hand with pain; and with hardship comes ease".
(Related by at-Tirmidhī)

Chapter 3

Virtues of seeking knowledge

It is reported that Qabīṣah ibn al-Mukhāriq (*r*) said: "I came to the Prophet (*ṣ*), and he asked me, 'What brings you here, Qabīṣah?'. I replied: 'I have grown old and my bones have grown weak, so I have come to you that you may teach me something by which Allah may benefit me'. He told me: 'O Qabīṣah, every stone, tree or piece of clay that you pass by asks Allah's forgiveness for you. Qabīṣah, when you have prayed the dawn prayer, say this three times: 'Most Glorified is Allah Almighty; all praise be to Him! (*Subḥāna Allāhi 'l-'Aẓīm wa bi-ḥamdih*)'. You will then by protected from blindness, leprosy and semi-paralysis. Qabīṣah, say: 'O Allah, I ask You of what You have. Grant me of Your generosity, cover me with Your mercy, and send down Your blessings upon me (*Allāhumma innī as'aluka mimmā 'indak, wa afiḍ 'alayya min faḍlik, wa 'nshur 'alayya min raḥmatik, wa anzil 'alayya min barakātik*)'".
(Related by Aḥmad ibn Ḥanbal)

The following *Ḥadīth* is from Abū d-Dardā' (*r*): "I heard the Messenger of Allah (*ṣ*) say: 'For him who seeks a road to knowledge, Allah eases a road to Paradise. The angels lower their wings to him who seeks knowledge, in satisfaction with what he is doing. All those in the Heavens and those on earth, even fishes in the water, seek forgiveness for the knowledgeable. In Allah's eyes, a knowledgeable person is as superior to an ordinary worshipper as the moon is superior in brilliance to the other heavenly bodies. The people of knowledge (*'ulamā'*) are the heirs of the Prophets. The Prophets did not bequeath a dirham or a dinar. They only left knowledge; and that is a great fortune for those who grasp it'".
(Related by Abū Dā'ūd, at-Tirmidhī, Ibn Mājah, Ibn Ḥibbān, and al-Bayhaqī)

It is reported that Ṣafwān ibn 'Aṣṣāl al-Murādī (*r*) said: "I went to see the Prophet (*ṣ*), and found him in the Mosque, reclining on a red cloak of his. I told him, 'Messenger of Allah, I have come seeking knowledge'. He replied: 'Welcome to the seeker of knowledge! The angels cover the seeker of knowledge with their wings. They crowd over one another until they reach the lower Heaven, because of their love for what he seeks'".
(Related by Aḥmad, aṭ-Ṭabarānī, Ibn Ḥibbān, and al-Ḥākim)

Chapter 4

Helping the distressed

Ibn 'Umar (may Allah be pleased with him and his father) reported that the Messenger of Allah (*ṣ*) said: "A Muslim is the brother of every Muslim. He may neither wrong him nor forsake him. Whoever helps his brother in need, Allah will help him in his need. Whoever delivers his brother from distress, Allah in return will save him from one of the terrors of the Day of Resurrection. Whoever shields his brother, Allah will shield him on the Day of Resurrection".
(Related by Muslim and al-Bukhārī)

Abū Hurayrah (*r*) reported that the Prophet (*ṣ*) said: "He who saves a Believer from one of the cares of this world, Allah will save him from one of the agonies of the Day of Resurrection. Whoever eases matters for someone suffering hardship, Allah will ease matters for him both in this world and in the Hereafter. Whoever protects a Muslim, Allah will protect him in this life and the Hereafter. Allah helps the Servant so long as the Servant helps his brother. For him who travels a road to knowledge Allah will ease a way to Paradise. Whenever a group of people gathers in one of the Houses of Allah Most High (mosques), reciting and studying together the Holy Book of Allah, Serenity descends upon them, Mercy covers them, angels hover all around them, and Allah mentions them amongst those in His Presence. He whose deeds keep him behind, his lineage will not advance him".
(Related by Muslim)

Chapter 5

The merits of prostration (*sujūd*) before Allah, the Exalted

Ma'dān ibn Abī Ṭalḥah (*r*) said: "I met Thawbān, the protégé (*mawlā*) of Allah's Messenger (*ṣ*), and asked him: 'Tell me about some action for me to perform, for which Allah would admit me to Paradise' (or he may have said 'about the most loved of actions [in the sight of Allah]'). [Thawbān] said nothing. I asked him again, and he remained silent. I then asked him a third time, and he replied: 'I asked the Prophet (*ṣ*) about that, and he told me: You must perform *sujūd* frequently, for whenever you perform a single prostration (*sajdah*) Allah thereby raises you one degree higher and removes one sin from your Record'".
(Related by Muslim, at-Tirmidhī, an-Nasā'ī, and Ibn Mājah)

According to 'Ubādah ibn aṣ-Ṣāmit (*r*), he heard the Prophet (*ṣ*) say: "When any Servant performs a *sajdah* before Allah, Allah records for him a good deed (*ḥasanah*) for it, erases one of his sins, and raises him by one degree; so endeavour to prostrate yourselves frequently".
(Related by Ibn Majah)

Hudhayfah (*r*) recounted that the Prophet (*ṣ*) declared: "There is no state in which a Servant [of Allah] could be dearer to Him than when Allah sees him in *sajdah*, covering his face with dust".
(Related by aṭ-Ṭabarānī)

Chapter 6

Merits of charity (*ṣadaqah*)

Ka'b ibn 'Ujrah (*r*) reported that the Messenger of Allah (*ṣ*) said: "O Ka'b ibn 'Ujrah, no flesh or blood grown on illicit gains will ever enter Paradise: Hell-Fire is more fitting for them. O Ka'b ibn 'Ujrah, there are two kinds of people. One kind aim to ransom their souls and so set them free; another kind put their souls in shackles. O Ka'b ibn 'Ujrah, prayer (*ṣalāt*) is a *qurbān* (a means of approaching Allah); fasting (*ṣawm*) is a shield; and charity (*ṣadaqah*) washes away sins as [easily as] ice slides over rocks".
(Related by Ibn Ḥibbān)

Mu'ādh ibn Jabal (*r*) stated, "I was with the Prophet (*ṣ*) on a journey", and narrated the same *Ḥadith* as above, but with the following difference: "He – meaning the Prophet (*ṣ*) – then said, 'Should I not guide you to the doors of Goodness (*khayr*)?'. I replied, 'Yes indeed, O Messenger of Allah'. He said: 'Fasting is a shield; and charity puts out sins just as water puts out fire'".
(Related by at-Tirmidhī)

"The Messenger of Allah (*ṣ*) said: 'Truly, charity quenches the burning of the grave for those who practise it. On the Day of Resurrection, the Believer will find shade only in the shadow of the charity that he gave'".
(Related by aṭ-Ṭabarānī and al-Bayhaqi)

Maymūnah bint Sa'd (*r*) narrated that she once asked: "O Messenger of Allah, give us your ruling about charity". He replied: "It is a shield against Hell-Fire for those who practise it with a view to the Hereafter, seeking only the Face of Allah Most Mighty and Glorious".
(Related by aṭ-Ṭabarānī)

Chapter 7

The merits of praying two *rak'ahs* in the forenoon (*aḍ-ḍuḥā)* and fasting three days each month

Abū Hurayrah (*r*) is reported to have said: "My dear friend [the Prophet], Allah's blessings and greetings be upon him, advised me to fast three days each month, to pray two *rak'ahs* [daily] in the forenoon, and to offer *witr* prayer [three *rak'ahs* or one, nightly] before going to bed". (Related in five *Ṣaḥīḥ* collections)

'Abd Allāh ibn 'Amr ibn al-'Āṣ (*r*) narrated that the Messenger of Allah (*ṣ*) said: "Fasting three days of each month is [equivalent to] fasting daily throughout one's life (*ṣawm ad-dahr*)".
(Related by al-Bukhari and Muslim. Allah confirmed this *Ḥadīth* in the Holy Qur'ān, *Surah* 6, verse 160: "Whoever brings forth a good deed shall have ten times as many to their credit", which makes one day worth ten [and hence three days worth thirty, making one month].)

According to Abū Dharr (*r*), the Messenger of Allah (*ṣ*) said: "*Ṣadaqah* is due on account of every joint of a person's body, each morning. Now, each *tasbīḥ* (saying '*Subhāna 'Llāh:* Glorified is Allah') is a *ṣadaqah*; each *taḥmīd* (saying '*al-Ḥamdu li 'Llāh*: Praise be to Allah') is a *ṣadaqah;* each *tahlīlah* (saying '*Lā ilāha illā 'Llāh:* There is no god but Allah') is a *ṣadaqah;* and each *takbīrah* (saying '*Allāhu Akbar:* Allah is Greatest') is a *ṣadaqah.* Also enjoining good is a *ṣadaqah*; and forbidding evil is a *ṣadaqah.* But two *rak'ahs* prayed in the forenoon will suffice".
(Related by Muslim)

According to 'Abd Allāh ibn 'Umar (may Allah be pleased with him and his father) a man asked the

Prophet (ṣ) about fasting, and he answered: "Always fast on the 'white days', three days of each month." (Related by Aḥmad, at-Tirmidhī, an-Nasā'ī, Ibn Mājah, and Ibn Khuzaymah.)

We are told by Jarīr (*r*) that the Prophet (ṣ) said: "Fasting three days a month [amounts to] fasting the whole year. These three days are "the white days (*ayyām al-bayḍ*)": the thirteenth, the fourteenth and the fifteenth of each month".
(Related by an-Nasā'ī and al-Bayhaqī.)

Chapter 8

Ṣalāt at-Tasābīḥ : a special prayer for the pious

'Ikrimah reported from Ibn 'Abbās (*r*) that the Prophet (*ṣ*) said to al-'Abbās ibn 'Abd al-Muṭṭalib: "O my uncle 'Abbās! Should I not be kind, generous and obliging to you? Should I not urge you to practise ten good habits for which, if you practise them, Allah will forgive all your sins – first and last, old and new, major and minor, inadvertent and deliberate, secret and visible? Ten habits: pray four *rak'ahs*, and in each recite *al-Fātiḥah* (the opening Chapter of the Holy Quran) and another Surah. When you finish reciting in the first *rak'ah*, remain standing and repeat these words [of glorification (*tasābīḥ*)] fifteen times: 'Glorified is Allah; praise be to Allah; there is no god but Allah; Allah is Most Great (*Subḥāna 'Llāhi, wa 'l-ḥamdu li-'Llāhi, wa lā ilāha illā 'Llāh, wa 'Llāhu Akbar*)'.

"Then bow down in your first *rukū'*. While you are in this position recite [those *tasābīḥ*] ten times. Then, raising your head from *rukū'*, recite [the *tasābīḥ*] ten times. Prostrate yourself, and whilst in *sajdah* recite them ten times. Then sit up from *sujūd* and while in the sitting position, recite [the *tasābīḥ*] ten times. Prostrate yourself once again, and recite them ten times. Then sit up again and recite them ten times.

"In each *rak'ah*, then, you recite [the *tasābīḥ*] seventy-five times. You should do the same in all four *rak'ahs*. If you can, offer this *tasābīḥ* prayer once every day. If you cannot, then offer it once every Friday. If you cannot, then offer it once every month. If you cannot, then offer

it once every year. If you cannot, then offer it once during your lifetime".
(Related by Abū Dā'ūd, Ibn Mājah, and Ibn Khuzaymah)

Chapter 9

Asking Allah for forgiveness and well-being

Al-'Abbās ibn 'Abd al-Muṭṭalib (*r*) is reported to have said: "I said to the Prophet (*ṣ*): 'O Messenger of Allah, teach me something to ask of Allah Most High'. He replied: 'Ask Allah for well-being'. I waited several days, then called on him again. 'O Messenger of Allah, tell me something to ask of Allah Most High', I said. He replied: 'O 'Abbās, uncle of the Messenger of Allah, ask Allah for well-being in this world and in the Hereafter'".
(Related by at-Tirmidhī)

The above prayer should take the form: "O Allah, we ask You for forgiveness and well-being in this world and the Hereafter (*Allāhumma innā nas'aluka 'l-'afwa wa 'l-'āfiyata fī 'd-dunyā wa 'l-ākhirah*)".

Here are some more prayers (*du'ā*'s) which the Prophet (*ṣ*) used to say and to teach his Companions (*r*). Ibn 'Umar (*r*) said: "It rarely happened that the Prophet (*ṣ*) left a gathering without saying: 'O Allah, put in our hearts a portion of fear with which You would help us to reach Paradise; and a portion of certainty (*yaqīn*) with which You make it easy for us to endure worldly disasters. O Allah, grant us the benefit of our hearing, sight and strength as long as You keep us alive; and make these outlast us. O Allah, contrive our vengeance upon those who oppress us, and give us victory over our enemies. O Allah, make not this world our greatest worry, nor the highest reach of our knowledge. O Allah, appoint not for us rulers who have no mercy upon us'".
(Related by at-Tirmidhī)

In Arabic, the above *du'ā'* should be pronounced like this: "*Allāhumma 'qsim lanā min khashyatika mā tubal-*

lighunā bihi jannatak, wa min al-yaqīni mā tuhawwanu bihi 'alaynā maṣa'ib ad-dunyā. Allāhumma matti'nā bi-asmā'inā wa abṣārinā wa quwwatinā mā aḥyaytanā, wa 'j'alhu 'l-wāritha minnā, wa 'j'al tha'ranā 'alà man ẓalamanā, wa 'nṣurnā 'alà man 'ādānā, wa lā taj'al id-dunyā akbara hamminā wa lā mablagha 'ilminā, wa lā tusalliṭ 'alaynā man lā yarḥamunā".

Abū Hurayrah (*r*) reported that the Prophet (*ṣ*) said: "Those who would delight in Allah Most High answering their prayers in times of difficulty and affliction should make many supplications (*du'ās*) in their times of ease". (Related by at-Tirmidhī)

Ibn Mas'ūd (*r*) said that the Prophet (*ṣ*) used to say: "O Allah, I ask You for guidance and piety, virtue and freedom from want". In Arabic: "*Allāhumma innī as'aluka 'l-hudā wa 't-tuqā, wa 'l-afāfah wa 'l-ghanā*".
(Related by Muslim)

According to Ṭāriq ibn Ashīm al-Ashja'ī, a Companion (*r*): "When a man embraced Islam, the Prophet (*ṣ*) would teach him how to perform prayers, then tell him to make the following supplication (*du'ā'*): "O Allah, forgive me, have mercy on me, guide me, grant me good health, and provide for me (*Allāhumma 'ghfir lī wa 'rḥamnī, wa 'hdinī, wa 'āfinī, wa 'rzuqnī*)".
(Related by Muslim)

In another version of the same *Ḥadīth*, Ṭāriq (*r*) said that when a man came and asked, "Messenger of Allah, how should I speak when asking something of my Lord?", the Prophet (*ṣ*) said, "Say, 'O Allah, forgive me, have mercy on me, guide me, grant me good health, and provide for me' (*Allāhumma 'ghfir lī wa 'rḥamnī, wa 'hdinī, wa 'āfinī, wa 'rzuqnī*). These words combine your [interests in] this world and the Next World".
(Related by Muslim)

Abū Hurayrah (*r*) reported that the Prophet (*ṣ*) used to say: "O Allah, set right my faith, which is the safeguard of my affairs; set right my worldly life, which I have to live; set right my life in the Hereafter, to which I shall be returned; make life a source of abundance for me in every

good; and make death a relief for me from all evil". (In Arabic: "*Allāhumma aṣliḥ lī dīnī 'l-ladhī huwa 'iṣmatu amrī, wa 'ṣliḥ lī ākhiratī 'l-latī fīhā ma'ādī, wa 'j'ali 'l-ḥayāta ziyādatan lī fī kulli khayr, wa 'j'ali 'l-mawta rāḥatan lī min kulli sharr*".)
(Related by Muslim)

Abū Umāmah (*r*) said: "The Prophet (*ṣ*) made many *du'ā*'s none of which we memorized, so we told him: 'O Messenger of Allah, you have made many *du'ā*'s, none of which we have memorized!'. The Prophet responded: 'Shall I teach you a prayer (*du'ā'*) which sums up all the rest? Say: O Allah, I ask You the best of what Your Prophet, Muhammad (*ṣ*), asked You for. I seek refuge with You from the worst of that against which Your Prophet Muhammad (*ṣ*) sought Your protection. You are the One to Whom we turn for help; and it is for You to provide it. There is no strength nor power except by Allah'. (In Arabic: '*Allāhumma as'aluka min khayri mā sa'alaka minhu Nabiyyuka Muḥammadun ṣallā 'Llāhu 'alayhi wa sallam. Wa a'ūdhu bika min sharri ma 'sta'ādhaka minhu Nabiyyuka Muḥammadun ṣallā 'Llāhu 'alayhi wa sallam. Wa Anta 'l-Musta'ānu, wa 'alayka 'l-balāgh, wa lā ḥawla wa lā quwwata illā bi 'Llāh)*'".
(Related by at-Tirmidhī)

Chapter 10

Virtues of fasting

Abū Umāmah (*r*) said: "I [once] asked, 'O Messenger of Allah (*ṣ*), tell me to do something'. He said: 'You must fast, for it has no equal [in goodness]'. Then I asked [again], 'O Messenger of Allah, tell me to do something'. He said: 'You must fast, for it has no equal [in goodness]'. I asked [yet again], 'O Messenger of Allah, tell me to do something'. He said: 'You must fast, for there is nothing like it [in goodness]'".
(Related by an-Nasā'ī and Ibn Khuzaymah)

Abū Sa'īd (*r*) narrated as follows: "The Prophet (*ṣ*) said: 'No Servant [of Allah] fasts one day for the sake of Allah Most High, without Allah distancing his face from Hell-Fire by the measure of seventy autumns [i.e. years' journey], for the sake of that day'".
(Related by al-Bukhārī, Muslim, at-Tirmidhī, and an-Nasā'ī)

Chapter 11

The merits of *tawbah* (turning to Allah in repentance)

According to al-Agharr ibn Yasār al-Muzanī (*r*), "The Messenger of Allah (*ṣ*) said: "O people, turn to Allah in repentance, and seek His forgiveness. Indeed, I make repentance a hundred times a day".
(Related by al-Bukhārī)

Abū Hurayrah (*r*) said, "I heard Allah's Messenger (*ṣ*) declare: 'By Allah, I seek Allah's forgiveness and turn to Him in repentance more than seventy times a day'".
(Related by al-Bukhārī)

Anas ibn Mālik (*r*), the servant of Allah's Messenger (*ṣ*), said, "The Messenger of Allah (*ṣ*) declared: 'Truly, Allah is more overjoyed at His servant's repentance than any of you would be if he stumbled upon his long-lost camel in the wilderness'".
(Related by Muslim and al-Bukhārī)

According to another version, he [*ṣ*] said: "Imagine one of you travelling in the desert on a camel. His camel darts away from him carrying all his food and drink, and he despairs of ever recovering the camel. He then comes to a tree and lies down in its shade, having given up all hope of his camel. While in that state, suddenly he finds his camel by his side, grasps its halter, and says in extreme joy: 'O Allah, You are my Servant and I am Your Lord!' – the mistake being due to his great joy. Truly, Allah's joy when His Servant repents is greater than that man's joy".
(Related by Muslim)

According to Abū Mūsà 'Abd Allāh ibn Qays al-Ash'arī (*r*), the Prophet (*ṣ*) declared: "Allah Most High will extend His Hand at night so that daytime sinners may turn to

Him in repentance, and He will extend His Hand in day-time that night-time sinners may turn to Him in repentance, until the sun rises from the west (on the Last Day)". (Related by Muslim)

Chapter 12

The Pillars of Islam

Mu'ādh ibn Jabal (*r*) said: "I was travelling with the Messenger of Allah (*ṣ*). One morning while riding close to him I said to him: 'O Messenger of Allah, tell me of some good deed whereby I may enter Paradise and be far removed from the Fire'. He replied: 'You have asked about a momentous matter. Truly it is easy for those for whom Allah Most High makes it easy: worship Allah and associate nothing with Him; maintain the ritual prayers; pay *zakāt;* fast Ramadan; and perform pilgrimage (*Ḥajj*) to the House [*Ka'bah*]'.

Then he [*ṣ*] added: 'Shall I guide you to the Gates of Goodness (*khayr*)?'. I said: 'Yes indeed, O Messenger of Allah'. He said: 'Fasting is a shield; charity extinguishes wrongs as water puts out fire; and [the other Gate is] a man's prayer (*ṣalāt*) in the depths of the night'. He [*ṣ*] then recited the Words of Allah [*Surah* 32, verses 16-17]: "Their bodies forsake their beds as they call on their Lord in fear and desire. And they give charity from the provision We have granted them. No soul knows what joys are hidden in store for them as reward for their deeds".

He [*ṣ*] then asked, 'Shall I tell you what is the essential thing, its pillar and its highest peak?'. I answered: 'Yes, O Messenger of Allah'. He said: "The essential thing is Islam; prayer (*ṣalāt*) is its pillar; and its highest peak is *jihād* (struggle in the cause of Islam)'. Then he said, 'Shall I tell you the basis of all this?'. I replied, 'Yes, O Messenger of Allah'. He said: 'Restrain this!', pointing to his tongue. I asked, 'Are we to be punished for what we say with it?'. He replied: 'Yes, by your mother's grief! Nothing will fling people down onto their faces in Hell except the harvests they reap with their tongues'."

(Related by Aḥmad, at-Tirmidhī, an-Nasā'ī, and Ibn Mājah)

Chapter 13

Kindness to Parents

Abu Hurayrah (*r*) reported that a man came to the Prophet (*ṣ*) and asked, "O Messenger of Allah, who is most entitled to good companionship from me?". [The Prophet] replied: "Your mother". The man asked: "Then who?". The Prophet said: "Your mother". The man asked: "Then who?". The Prophet repeated, "Your mother". The man asked: "Then who?". The Prophet said: "Your father".
(Related by Muslim and al-Bukhārī)

In another version of the same *Ḥadīth*, the question was: "O Messenger of Allah, who is most entitled to good companionship?", and the reply: "Your mother; then your mother; then your mother; then your father; then your kin, in order of nearness".
(Related by Muslim)

Abū Hurayrah (*r*) also narrated that the Prophet (*ṣ*) said: "Rubbed in dust is the nose, rubbed in dust is the nose, rubbed in dust is the nose of him [meaning, 'Shame and disgrace on him'] who is alive when one or both of his parents reach old age – and who then fails to enter Paradise [by serving them and showing them kindness and compassion]".
(Related by Muslim)

Chapter 14

Performing Ritual Prayer (*ṣalāt*) regularly

According to ‘Abd Allāh ibn ‘Umar (*r*), the Prophet (*ṣ*) spoke one day about ritual prayer. He said: “It will be Light, Evidence, and Salvation on the Day of Resurrection, for those who perform it regularly. For those who do not, there will be no Light, Evidence, or Salvation: on the Day of Resurrection they will be with [sinners like] Qārūn, Pharaoh, Hāmān, and Ubayy ibn Khalaf”.
(Related by Aḥmad ibn Ḥanbal)

Anas (*r*) said: “Regular prayers were made obligatory upon the Prophet (*ṣ*) on the Night of *Isrā’* (his Ascension to the Heavens). They were fifty [prayers daily], but were then reduced until they were fixed as five. Then came the [Divine] Call: ‘O Muḥammad, there is no changing My Word. For these five [prayers] you shall have [the reward of] fifty’”.
(Related by Muslim, al-Bukhārī, Ibn Mājah, and at-Tirmidhī)

According to Abū Qatādah (*r*), the Prophet (*ṣ*) reported that Allah, the Almighty, the All-Glorious, said: “I prescribed for your Nation (*Ummah*) five [daily] prayers. I made a covenant with Myself to admit to Paradise those who come to Me having offered those five prayers regularly and at their appointed times. As for those who have not done so, they have no such covenant from Me”.
(Related by Abū Dā’ūd)

Abū Hurayrah (*r*) reported that the Prophet (*ṣ*) asked, “Imagine – if one of you had a river running right at his door, in which he washed five times every day, would any dirt would remain on him?”. [The Companions] said: “No dirt would remain on him”. The Prophet said: “Well, that is what the five prayers are like: with them Allah wipes out wrong actions”.
(Related by Muslim, al-Bukhārī, Ibn Mājah, and at-Tirmidhī)

‘Amr ibn Sa‘īd (*r*) said: “I was in the presence of ‘Uthmān (*r*). He prayed for purity, and said, ‘I heard the Messenger of Allah (*ṣ*) say: When the time for a prescribed prayer comes, if a Muslim performs *wuḍū* (ablution), prays and bows properly and humbly, that prayer invariably expiates all his past sins, so long as he does not commit major sins (*kabā’ir*); and this holds good for all time’”.
(Related by Muslim)

‘Uthmān ibn ‘Affān (*r*) reported that he heard the Prophet (*ṣ*) say: “Praying the night prayer (*‘ishā’*) in a group (*jamā‘ah*) is like praying half the length of all the night. Praying *fajr* (dawn prayer) in a group is like praying all night long”.
(Related by Muslim)

Abū Mūsā (*r*) reported that the Messenger of Allah (*ṣ*) declared: “He who prays in the two cool times (*fajr* and *‘aṣr*) will enter Paradise”.
(Related by Muslim and al-Bukhārī)

Chapter 15

Good Character

Abū 'd-Dardā' (*r*) reported that Allah's Messenger (*ṣ*) said: "On the Day of Resurrection, nothing will weigh better in the Scales for any of Allah's Servants (true Believers) than good character. Truly Allah detests the wicked and the foul-tongued".
(Related by Abū Dā'ūd and at-Tirmidhī)

Abū Hurayrah (*r*) reported that the Messenger of Allah (*ṣ*) said: "Amongst the Believers, the most perfect in faith (*īmān*) is the best in conduct; and the best of you are those who are best to their families".
(Related by Abū Dā'ūd and at-Tirmidhī)

Jābir (*r*) related that the Messenger of Allah (*ṣ*) said: "The best of you in character will be among the best-loved and those stationed closest to me on the Day of Judgement. The prattlers, the braggarts, and the *mutafayhiqūn* will be the most detested by me and those stationed farthest from me on the Day of Resurrection". [The Companions] enquired, "Who are the *mutafayhiqūn*?". He replied, "The arrogant".
(Related by at-Tirmidhī)

Chapter 16

What should be said after every prayer (*ṣalāt*)

Mu'ādh ibn Jabal (*r*) reported that Allah's Messenger (*ṣ*) once grasped his hand and said: "O Mu'ādh, by Allah I truly love you!" Mu'ādh replied, "You are as a father and mother to me, O Messenger of Allah, and by Allah I truly love you!" He said, "I advise you, Mu'ādh, to be sure to say these words after every prayer (*ṣalāt*): 'O Allah, help me ever to remember, praise and worship You well (*Allāhumma a'innī 'alà dhikrika wa shukrika wa ḥusni 'ibādatik*)'".
(Related by Abū Dā'ūd, an-Nasā'ī, Ibn Khuzaymah, and Ibn Ḥibban)

Abū Hurayrah (*r*) reported that Allah's Messenger (*ṣ*) said: "He who after each prayer glorifies Allah [saying 'Exalted is Allah: *Subḥāna 'Llāh*'] thirty-three times; praises Allah [saying 'Praise be to Allah: *al-Ḥamdu li-'Llāh*'] thirty-three times; and extols His Greatness [saying 'Allah is Most Great: *Allāhu Akbar*'] thirty-three times, making ninety-nine in all; then adds, to complete the hundred, 'There is no god but Allah, He has no associates, to Him belongs the whole universe and to Him alone all praise is due, and He is the Omnipotent Who has power over all things (*Lā ilāha illā 'Llāh, waḥdahu lā sharīka lah, lahu 'l-mulku wa lahu 'l-ḥamd, wa Huwa 'alā kulli shay'in Qadīr*)' – his wrong actions will be forgiven him, even if they be as [much as] the foam of the sea".
(Related by Muslim)

Sa'd ibn Abī Waqqāṣ (*r*) reported that the Messenger of Allah (*ṣ*) used to seek refuge with these words after prayer (*ṣalāt*): "O Allah, I seek refuge with You from cowardice and miserliness; I seek refuge with You from

feebleness in old age; I seek refuge with You from the trials of this world (*dunyà*); and I seek refuge with You from the trials of the grave (*Allāhumma innī a'ūdhu bika min al-jubni wa 'l-bukhl, wa a'ūdhu bika an uradda ilà ardhali 'l-'umr, wa a'ūdhu bika min fitnati 'd-dunyà, wa a'udhu bika min fitnati 'l-qabr*)".
(Related by al-Bukhārī)

The Mother of the Believers Juwayriyyah bint al-Ḥārith (*r*) reported that one day the Prophet (*ṣ*) left her in the morning, after *ṣalāt*, sitting in her place of prayer (*masjid*). When he returned after forenoon began, he found her still sitting there. He asked: "Are you still in the same state in which I left you?" "Yes", she replied. The Prophet (*ṣ*) then said: "After I left you, I spoke four phrases three times; if they were weighed against all that you have said today, they would outweigh it all: 'Glory and Praise be to Allah, as many times as the number of His creatures and creation, as much as pleases Him, as heavy in the Scale as His Throne, and as infinite as the ink required to record His Words (*Subḥāna 'Llāhi 'l-'Aẓīmi wa biḥamdih, 'adada khalqihi wa riḍā'a Nafsih, wa zinata 'Arshih, wa midāda Kalimātih*)'".
(Related by Muslim)

Chapter 17

Excellence of *dhikr* (remembrance, or invocation, of Allah)

'Abd Allah ibn Busr (*r*) reported that a man said, "O Messenger of Allah, the Laws of Islam are too many for me, so tell me something that I may cling to". He [*ṣ*] replied: "Let your tongue never cease to be moist from invoking Allah".
(Related by al-Tirmidhī, Ibn Mājah, al-Ḥākim, and Ibn Ḥibbān)

According to Mu'ādh (*r*), a man asked the Prophet (*ṣ*): "Which *mujāhid* (striver in the cause of Allah) will receive the greatest reward?". [The Prophet] replied: "The one who remembers Allah (Blessed and Exalted is He) the most". The man asked: "Which righteous person will receive the highest reward?" The Prophet replied: "The one who remembers Allah (Blessed and Exalted is He) the most." The man repeated the same question, mentioning prayer (*ṣalāt*), the poor tax (*zakāt*), the Pilgrimage (*ḥajj*), and charity (*ṣadaqah*). Each time the Messenger of Allah replied, "The one who remembers Allah (Blessed and Exalted is He) the most". Then Abū Bakr said to 'Umar: "O Abū Ḥafṣ, those who remember Allah have carried off all the goodness!" The Messenger of Allah remarked: "Yes indeed!"
(Related by Aḥmad ibn Ḥanbal and aṭ-Ṭabarānī)

Chapter 18

Personal qualities

Zayd al-Khayr (*r*) related that he once said to the Prophet (*ṣ*), "Messenger of Allah, surely you will tell me what are the signs of those whom Allah likes and of those whom He dislikes?". [The Prophet (*ṣ*)] asked him, "What about you, Zayd?". Zayd replied, "I love goodness (*khayr*) and those who do it. I hasten to do good whenever I can; if I miss an opportunity, I am sad and long to find another". [The Prophet (*ṣ*)] then observed, "Well, those are the qualities of those whom Allah likes. Had He intended anything else for you, He would have made you different". (Related by Razīn)

Abū Ayyūb (*r*) related that the Messenger of Allah (*ṣ*) said, "Four of the habitual practices (*Sunan*) of the Prophets are modesty, the use of perfume, marriage, and brushing the teeth (*siwāk*)".
(Related by at-Tirmidhī)

Abū Hurayrah (*r*) reported that Allah's Messenger (*ṣ*) asked, "Shall I tell you who are the best among you and who are the worst?". He repeated the question three times, and they [the Companions] replied "Yes indeed". He said, "The best of you are those from whom good can be expected and there is an assurance of no evil from him. The worst are those from whom no good can be expected and from whom there can be no assurance that he will not do evil".
(Related by at-Tirmidhī)

Abū Bakrah (*r*) related that the Messenger of Allah (*ṣ*) was once asked, "Which people are best?". He replied: "Those whose lives are long and their actions good". Someone asked, "And which people are worst?". He replied: "Those whose lives are long and their actions bad".
(Related by at-Tirmidhī)

Chapter 19

Renouncing acts of disobedience to Allah, and adhering to obedience to and remembrance of Him

Umm Anas (*r*) narrated that she once said: "O Messenger of Allah, advise me!" He said: "Renounce all sins, for they are the best to forsake. Adhere to obligatory duties, for they are the best form of *jihād*. Remember Allah a great deal, for there is no better [deed] with which to meet Allah".

It is related from Abū Hurayrah (*r*) that the Messenger of Allah (*ṣ*) said: "Allah Almighty says: 'I am as My servant considers Me to be, and I am with him when he mentions Me. If he mentions Me to himself, I mention him to Myself; if he mentions Me in an assembly, I will mention him in a better Assembly. If he draws a hand's span nearer to Me, I draw an arm's length nearer to him; and if he draws an arm's length nearer to Me, I draw a fathom nearer to him. And if he comes walking towards Me, I go towards him at speed'".
(Related by al-Bukhārī, Muslim and at-Tirmidhī)

Accordance to Mu'āwiyah (*r*), the Messenger of Allah (*ṣ*) once passed a group of his Companions sitting in a circle and asked them: "Why are you sitting here?". They replied: "We have gathered to invoke Allah, praising Him for guiding us to Islam and for all that He granted us". He asked: "By Allah, are you here for that reason only?". They replied: "By Allah, we are here only for that". [The Prophet (*ṣ*)] said: "I assure you, I did not adjure you out of any suspicion of you; but Gabriel came to me and told me that Allah is speaking proudly of you to the angels".
(Related by Muslim, al-Bukhārī, and an-Nasā'ī)

Chapter 20

Excellence of the two *rak'ah*s [before] the dawn (*fajr*) prayer

It is narrated from Ibn 'Umar (*r*) that a man once said: "O Messenger of Allah, tell me of some action by which Allah will grant me benefit". [The Prophet (*ṣ*)] replied: "Be sure to offer the two [*Sunnah*] *rak'ahs* [before] the *fajr* (dawn) prayer: there is [great] merit in them".
(Related by aṭ-Ṭabarānī)

Another narration, also from Ibn 'Umar (*r*): "I heard Allah's Messenger (*ṣ*) say, "Do not omit the two *rak'ahs* before the *fajr* prayer, for they contain all that one could wish for".

It was reported by 'Ā'ishah (*r*) that the Prophet (*ṣ*) said: "The two [*Sunnah*] *rak'ahs* of *fajr* are better than this world and all that is in it".

In another version, from Muslim: "They are dearer to me that the whole world".
(Related by Muslim and at-Tirmidhī)

Chapter 21

Avoid being distracted during prayer (*ṣalāt*)

Anas (*r*) related that the Messenger of Allah (*ṣ*) said: "My dear son, be sure to avoid being distracted during prayer: to become distracted while praying is a disaster!"
(Related by at-Tirmidhī)

Abū Hurayrah (*r*) reported: "The Messenger of Allah (*ṣ*) said: 'When a servant [of Allah] stands in prayer' – I think he said – 'he stands before none other than the All-Merciful, Blessed and Exalted is He. If he becomes distracted, Allah (Blessed and Exalted is He) says: 'Whom are you thinking of instead? Someone better than Me? O son of Adam, come to Me: I am Better than the one of whom you are thinking'".
(Related by al-Bazzār)

Chapter 22

The merit of true sincerity (*ikhlāṣ*)

Mu'ādh ibn Jabal (*r*) recounted that when he was sent (as Governor) to Yemen he said, "Messenger of Allah, advise me". [The Prophet] (*ṣ*) told him: "Make your faith (*dīn*) pure; then even a few actions will suffice you".
(Related by al-Ḥākim)

Thawbān narrated: "I heard the Messenger of Allah (*ṣ*) say, "Blessed are the pure of faith: they are the guiding lights. For them all the darkness of tribulation will be dispelled".
(Related by al-Bayhaqī)

Abū 'Umāmah (*r*) reported that the Prophet (*ṣ*) said: "Allah Most Mighty and Glorious accepts only those actions that are performed sincerely and for His sake alone".
(Related by Abū Dā'ūd and an-Nasā'ī)

Chapter 23

For those who have a special need to ask from Allah

'Abd Allāh ibn Abī 'Awfā (*r*) reported that the Messenger of Allah (*ṣ*) said: "He who has a need of Allah or of any of the Children of Adam should perform a thorough ablution (*wuḍū'*) and offer two *rak'ah*s of prayer. He should then praise Allah and invoke His blessings upon the Prophet (*ṣ*).

After that, he should say: 'There is no God but Allah, the Forbearing, the Generous. Exalted is Allah, Lord of the Mighty Throne. Praise be to Allah, Lord of the Worlds. O Allah, I ask You [to guide me to] deeds that bring Your mercy and forgiveness. I ask You for protection against committing any sin; for the benefit of performing all acts of virtue (*birr*); and for safety from doing any wrong. Leave no sin of mine unforgiven, no trouble of mine unrelieved, and satisfy all my needs that it pleases You to meet, O Most Merciful of the merciful.'"

The *du'ā'* in Arabic: '*Lā ilāha illā 'Llāhu 'l-Ḥalīmu 'l-Karīm. Subḥāna 'Llāhi Rabbi 'l-'arshi 'l-'aẓīm. Al-Ḥamdu li 'Llāhi Rabbi 'l-'ālamīn. As'aluka mūjibāti rahmatika wa 'azā'ima maghfiratik, wa 'l-'iṣmata min kulli dhanb, wa 'l-ghanīmata min kulli birr, wa 's-salāmata min kulli ithm. La taḍa' lī dhanban illā ghafartah, wa lā hamma illā farrajtah, wa lā ḥājatan hiya laka riḍā'an illā qaḍaytah, yā Arḥama 'r-rāḥimīn*'.

(Related by at-Tirmidhī and Ibn Mājah)

Ibn Mājah adds the following, after 'O Most Merciful of the merciful': "Then he may ask whatever he wishes in matters of this world or the Hereafter, and so they will be decreed".

Prayer for the granting of a need (*ṣalāt al-ḥājah*), and the supplication for it

According to ‘Uthmān ibn Ḥanīf, a blind man came to Allah’s Messenger (ṣ) and said, “O Messenger of Allah, pray to Allah that He may remove the veil from my eyesight”. He answered, “Or shall I show you how to do the prayer?”. The man said, “O Messenger of Allah, the loss of my sight has caused me much grief!”. [The Prophet (s)] told him, “Go and perform ablution (*wuḍū*), and pray two *rak‘ah*s. Then say, ‘O Allah, I ask You and turn to You for the sake of my Prophet Muḥammad (ṣ), the Prophet of Mercy. O Muḥammad, I turn to my Lord that for your sake He may restore my sight. O Allah, let him intercede for me, and let me intercede for myself’.” Later the man came back. Allah had restored his sight.
(Related by at-Tirmidhī, an-Nasā’ī, Ibn Mājah, Ibn Khuzaymah, and al-Ḥākim)

Chapter 24

Moral Maladies

Abū Dharr (*r*) reported that Allah's Messenger (*ṣ*) said: "There are three types of people whom Allah will neither speak to nor even look at on the Day of Resurrection. He will not purify them, and theirs will be a painful chastisement". He repeated that three times. [Abū Dharr] then asked: "O Messenger of Allah, they have failed and lost everything! Who are they?". He answered: "Those who trail [their garments from arrogance], those who impose obligation [in return for gifts or kindnesses], and those who make their merchandise more saleable by swearing false oaths".
(Related in five collections, al-Bukhārī being the exception)

According to Abū Barzah al-Aslamī (*r*), the Prophet (*ṣ*) said: "What I most fear for you are the excessive appetites of your stomachs and private parts, and trials that tempt you to go astray".
(Related by Razīn)

Jābir ibn 'Abd Allāh al-Anṣārī (*r*) reported that the Messenger of Allah (*ṣ*) said: "Beware of committing oppression (*ẓulm*)! Oppression becomes manifold darkness (*ẓulumāt*) on the Day of Judgement. Beware, too of avarice! Avarice destroyed those who lived before you: it led them to shed one another's blood and to consider lawful what was forbidden them".
(Related by Muslim)

According to Jundub (*r*), Allah's Messenger (*ṣ*) said, "Whoever speaks of someone's unknown faults, Allah will speak of his; and whoever makes them visible, Allah will do the same to him".
(Related by al-Bukhāri and Muslim)

Chapter 25

On helping those who ask something by Allah, the Mighty and Glorious

Jābir (*r*) – and, in another text, Ibn 'Umar (*r*) – narrated that the Messenger of Allah (*ṣ*) said: "If someone seeks refuge "by Allah", offer him refuge and protection. If someone asks something by Allah, give him what he asks for. If someone calls you, respond to his call. If someone does you a favour, reward him. If you have nothing to reward him with, pray for him until you see that you have offered him an adequate reward".
(Related by Abū Dā'ūd, an-Nasā'ī, and Ibn Ḥibbān)

The prohibition of asking for the sake of Allah

Rāfi' (*r*) reported that the Messenger of Allah (*ṣ*) said: "Accursed is he who asks 'for the sake of Allah' (*li-Wajh Allāh*); and accursed is he who is asked 'for the sake of Allah' and turns away the one who asked".
(Related by aṭ-Ṭabarānī)

Note. There is no contradiction in these *Hadīth*s. It is sinful to ask for something 'for the sake of Allah'; but if someone does so and you are able to give it then you may not refuse.

Chapter 26

The excellence of "The Mother of the Book" (*Sūrat al-Fātiḥah*, the first chapter of Qur'ān)

Abū Hurayrah (*r*) reported that he heard the Prophet (*ṣ*) say: "Allah Most Exalted has said: 'I have divided prayer (*ṣalāt*) between Myself and My servant into two halves [one version of the *Ḥadīth* adds, 'one half for Me and one half for My servant']. My servant shall have what he has asked for. When the servant says: 'All praise is for Allah, Lord of the Universe (*al-Ḥamdu li 'Llāhi Rabbi 'l-'ālamīn*)', Allah says: 'My servant has praised Me'. When he says: 'the All-Merciful, the Compassionate (*ar-Raḥmāni 'r-Raḥīm*)', Allah says: 'My servant has extolled Me'. When he says: 'Master of the Day of Judgement (*Māliki yawmi 'd-Dīn*), Allah says 'My servant has glorified Me'. When he says: 'You alone do we worship and ask for help (*iyyāka na'budu wa iyyāka nasta'īn*)', He says: 'This is between Me and My servant, and My servant shall have what he has asked for'. When he says: 'Guide us on the straight path; the path of those whom You have blessed, not of those on whom Anger falls, nor of them that are astray (*ihdinā 's-ṣirāṭa 'l-mustaqīm, ṣirāṭa 'l-ladhīna an'amta 'alayhim, ghayri 'l-maghḍūbi 'alayhim, wa lā 'ḍ-ḍāllīn*)', He says: 'This is for My servant, and My servant shall have what he has asked for'".
(Related by Muslim)

Abu Sa'īd ibn al-Mu'allā (*r*) said: "Once I was praying in the Mosque when the Messenger of Allah (*ṣ*) called me, so I did not answer him. Then I came to him and said: 'O Messenger of Allah, I was praying'. He replied: 'Has not Allah said, Answer the call of Allah and of the

Messenger when he summons you?' Then he said, 'Before you leave this mosque I will surely tell you of a *Surah* which is the mightiest *Sūrah* of the Qur'ān'. He then grasped my hand. Later, when we wanted to leave the mosque, I said: 'O Messenger of Allah, you said, I will surely tell you of a *Sūrah* which is the mightiest *Sūrah* of the Qur'ān'. [The Prophet (ṣ)] told me, 'It is: All praise is for Allah, Lord of the Universe (*al-Ḥamdu li 'Llāhi Rabbi 'l-'ālamīn*), the seven oft-repeated [verses], by the Glorious Qur'ān that has been granted to me'."
(Related by al-Bukhārī, Abū Dā'ūd, an-Nasā'ī, and Ibn Mājah)

Chapter 27

Concerning the excellence of certain Qur'ānic *Sūrahs* and verses

Anas (*r*) recounted that the Messenger of Allah (*ṣ*) asked a man, one of his Companions, "Are you married?". He answered: "No, by Allah, O Messenger of Allah. I cannot afford it". [The Prophet (*ṣ*)] said: "Do you not know 'Say, He, Allah, is One (*Qul Huwa 'Llāhu Aḥad*)' [*Sūrah* 112]?". He said: "Yes, I do". He [*ṣ*] said: "This is one-third of the Qur'ān! Do you not know 'When Allah's help comes, and victory (*Idhā jā'a naṣru 'Llāhi wa 'l-fatḥ*)' [*Sūrah* 110]?" The man said: "Yes". [The Prophet (*ṣ*)] said: "This is a quarter of the Qur'ān! Do you not know 'Say, O unbelievers (*Qul yā ayyuhā 'l-kāfirūn*)' [*Sūrah* 109]?". The man replied: "Yes". [The Prophet (*ṣ*)] said "This is a quarter of the Qur'ān! Do you not know 'When the Earth is made to quake (*Idhā zulzilati 'l-arḍ*)' [*Sūrah* 99]?". "Yes", replied the man. [The Prophet (*ṣ*)] said: "This is a quarter of the Qur'ān! Get married, get married!". (Related by at-Tirmidhī)

The excellence of *Sūrat al-Ikhlāṣ* (112), the end of *Sūrat al-Baqarah* (2), and the Throne Verse (2:255)

Mu'ādh ibn Anas al-Juhanī (*r*) related that the Messenger of Allah (*ṣ*) said: "For one who recites the entire *Sūrah* 'Qul Huwa 'Llāhu Aḥad (*Sūrah* 112)' ten times, a palace will be built in Paradise". 'Umar ibn al-Khaṭṭāb (*r*) then said, "In that case we will try to do so many times (*nastakthir*), O Messenger of Allah!". The Messenger of

Allah (*ṣ*) replied, "Allah is More (*akthar*) and Finer (*aṭyab*) [than that reward]".
(Related by Aḥmad ibn Ḥanbal)

Abū Dharr (*r*) related that Allah's Messenger (*ṣ*) remarked: "Allah has concluded *Sūrat al-Baqarah (Surah* 2) with two *āyahs* (verses) which He granted me from the Treasure beneath the [Divine] Throne. So learn them, and teach them to your womenfolk and children: they are prayer (*ṣalāt*), Qur'ān, and supplication (*du'ā*)".
(Related by al-Ḥākim)

'Ā'ishah (*r*) reported that the Prophet (*ṣ*) sent a man on a raiding party. Leading his companions in prayer, the man always ended by reciting *'Qul Huwa 'Llāhu Aḥad (Sūrah* 112)'. On their return, they mentioned this to the Prophet (*ṣ*). He said: "Ask him why he does so", so they asked him. The man replied, "Because it describes the All-Merciful and I love reciting it". [When he heard this] the Prophet said, "Tell him that Allah loves him".
(Related by al-Bukhārī, Muslim, and an-Nasā'ī)

Abū Hurayrah (*r*) related: "The Messenger of Allah (*ṣ*) once appointed me to look after the *zakāt* given during Ramadan. [One night] someone came and tried to make off with some of the food. I caught him and told him, 'I will definitely hand you over to the Messenger of Allah (*ṣ*)'. [The culprit] said, 'I am in need: I have dependants to look after, and I need it badly', so I let him go. Next morning, Allah's Messenger (*ṣ*) asked me, 'Abū Hurayrah, what did your captive do last night?' I replied, 'O Messenger of Allah, he complained about his need and his dependants, so I had mercy on him and let him go on his way'. [The Prophet (*ṣ*)] said: 'But he lied to you, and he will come back again'.

"I knew, therefore, that [that person] would return as the Messenger of Allah (*ṣ*) had said, so I lay in wait for him. He came back and tried to make off with some food. I said, 'I will definitely hand you over to the Messenger of Allah (*ṣ*). He said, 'Let me go. I am in need and I have dependants. I will not come back'. So I had mercy on him and let him go on his way. Next morning, the Messenger of of Allah (ṣ) asked me, 'Abū Hurayrah, what did your captive do last night?'. I replied, 'O Messenger of Allah, he complained about his need and his dependants, so I had mercy on him and let him go on his way'. [The Prophet (ṣ)] said: 'But he lied to you, and he will come back again'.

"I therefore lay in wait for him a third time. He came back and tried to make off with some food. I caught him yet again and told him, 'I will definitely take you to the Prophet. This is the third and last time that you promised not to return, then came back'. He said 'Release me and I will teach you words by which Allah will benefit you'. I said, 'What are they?' He said, 'When you go to bed, recite *Āyat al-Kursī* (the Throne Verse: *Sūrah* 2, verse 255). You will then be under constant protection by Allah and no devil will approach you until morning'. So I let him go on his way. Next morning the Messenger of Allah (ṣ) asked me: 'What did your captive do last night?'. I replied, 'Messenger of Allah, he claimed that he would teach me words by which Allah would benefit me, so I let him go on his way'. He asked, 'What words?'. I said, 'He told me, When you go to bed, recite *Āyat al-Kursī,* from beginning (*Allāhu lā ilāha illā Huwa 'l-Ḥayyu 'l-Qayyūm*) to the end. You will then be under constant protection by Allah and no devil will approach you until morning.' The Prophet (ṣ) said, 'This time he told you the truth, even though he is a great liar. Do you know whom you were speaking with these last three nights, Abū Hurayrah?'. 'No', I replied. He said 'That was a devil (*shayṭān*)!'." (Related by al-Bukhārī)

Ubayy ibn Ka'b (*r*) reported that his father told him that they had a small barn for drying and storing dates; [Ka'b, his father] was under contract [to store them]. [Once] he found that they were diminishing in number, and so he began to keep watch over the barn at night. Suddenly [one night] there appeared a creature whose form resembled that of an adolescent young man. According to [Ubayy], [Ka'b] greeted him, and he returned the greeting. [Ka'b] then asked: "Which are you: jinn or human?" "Jinn" was the reply. "Show me your hand",

demanded [Ka'b]. It was a dog's paw, with dog's hair. "That is a jinn's physique", said [Ka'b]. "The jinn know that none of them is stronger than I", remarked the jinn. "What led you to do what you did?" asked [Ka'b]. The jinn answered: "I was told that you like giving charity, so I wanted to have some food of yours". "What can protect us from you [jinns]?" asked [Ka'b]. "This verse: —*Ayat al-Kursī*", said the jinn. Ka'b said that he then left the jinn. "Early next day", Ubayy reported, "My father went to the Messenger of Allah (*ṣ*) and told him of the incident. [The Prophet (*ṣ*)] said: 'The wicked one spoke the truth'."
(Related by Ibn Ḥibbān and others)

Merits of *Sūrat al-Ikhlāṣ* (112) and *al-Mu'awwidhatān* (113 and 114)

Mu'ādh ibn 'Abd Allāh ibn Khubayb reported that his father (*r*) said: "One very dark and rainy night, we were looking for the Messenger of Allah (*ṣ*) to lead us in prayer. When we found him he told me: 'Say something'. I did not say anything. He repeated: 'Say something'. Still I said nothing. Yet again he repeated: 'Say something'. I said: 'O Messenger of Allah, what should I say?' He replied: '*Qul Huwa 'Llāhu Aḥad,* and the two Refuge-Seekers (*al-Mu'awwidhatān*: Sūrahs 113 and 114) three times each morning and evening. They will suffice you in all respects'".
(Related by Abū Dā'ūd and at-Tirmidhī)

'Uqbah ibn 'Āmir (*r*) reported that the Messenger of Allah (*ṣ*) said: "Do you not know of some verses which were revealed at night, the like of which have never been seen? [They are] *Qul a'ūdhu bi-Rabbi 'l-falaq* and *Qul a'ūdhu bi-Rabbi 'n-nās* (*Sūrahs* 113 and 114)".
(Related by Muslim, at-Tirmidhī, an-Nasā'ī, and Abū Dā'ūd)

In another version of the same *Ḥadīth*, 'Uqbah (*r*) said: "I was guiding the Messenger of Allah (*ṣ*) on a journey,

when he asked, "Uqbah, shall I teach you the two best *Sūrahs* ever recited?'. He then taught me '*Qul a'ūdhu bi-Rabbi 'l-falaq*' [*Sūrah* 113] and '*Qul a'ūdhu bi-Rabbi 'n-nās*' [*Sūrah* 114]".
(Related by Muslim, at-Tirmidhī, an-Nasā'ī, and Abū Dā'ud)

Another version: "Once I was travelling with the Messenger of Allah (*ṣ*) between al-Juḥfah and al-Abwā' when a wind and extreme darkness overcame us. This led the Messenger of Allah (*ṣ*) to seek refuge by means of '*A'ūdhu bi-Rabbi 'l-falaq*' and '*A'ūdhu bi-Rabbi 'n-Nās*'. He said, "Uqbah, seek refuge by these two [*Sūrahs*]: for those seeking refuge, there is no means superior to them'." ['Uqbah] added, "And I heard him entrust us to their protection during the prayer (*ṣalāt*)".
(Related by Abū Dā'ūd)

Jābir ibn 'Abd Allāh (*r*) reported: The Messenger of Allah (*ṣ*) once told him: "Jābir, recite". "What should I recite, O you who are like a father and mother to me?" I asked. He said: "'*Qul a'ūdhu bi-Rabbi 'l-falaq*' and '*Qul a'ūdhu bi-Rabbi 'n-nas*'; so I recited them. Then he [*ṣ*] said: 'Recite them both. There is nothing else like them that you could recite'."
(Related by an-Nasā'ī and Ibn Ḥibbān)

Chapter 28

Reviving a practice (*Sunnah*) of the Prophet (*ṣ*)

'Amr ibn 'Awf (*r*) reported that one day the Prophet (*ṣ*) told Bilāl ibn al-Ḥārith, "Know, O Bilāl". "What must I know, O Messenger of Allah?", he asked. [The Prophet (*ṣ*)] replied, "Know that anyone who revives one *Sunnah* (practice) of mine that has fallen into disuse after my lifetime will get as much reward as those who will follow that *Sunnah*, without their reward being diminished in the least. And anyone who introduces a misguided innovation with which neither Allah nor His Messenger are pleased will bear as many sins as those who act on their innovations, without those people's burden of guilt being diminished in the least."
(Related by at-Tirmidhī and Ibn Mājah)

Ibn 'Abbās (*r*) also reported that the Prophet (*ṣ*) said: "One who holds fast to my *Sunnah* when my Nation (*Ummah*) is corrupt will have the reward of a hundred martyrs."
(Related by al-Bayhaqī and aṭ-Ṭabarānī)

Chapter 29

Renunciation of worldly things (*Zuhd ad-dunyā*)

Abū ʻAbbās Sahl ibn Saʻd as-Sāʻidī (*r*) reported: "A man came to the Prophet (*ṣ*) and said to Him: 'Messenger of Allah, guide me to some action for which Allah and people would love me'. He replied: 'Renounce worldly things, and Allah will love you. Renounce the things that people possess, and they will love you'".
(Related by Ibn Mājah and others)

The detachment of our Master, Allah's Messenger (*ṣ*), from worldly things

According to ʻAbd Allāh ibn Masʻūd (*r*): "The Messenger of Allah (*ṣ*) used to sleep on a simple straw mat. When he got up, the mat left its mark on his side. We said: 'O Messenger of Allah, what if we were to get you a carpet?' He answered: 'What have I to do with this world? In this world I am but a rider who rests in the shade of a tree, then sets off and leaves it behind'".
(Related by at-Tirmidhī)

Being content with what one has (*qanāʻah*)

ʻUbayd Allāh ibn Muḥṣin al-Anṣārī al-Khuṭamī (*r*) reported that the Messenger of Allah (*ṣ*) said: "For those of you who wake up in the morning safe in their flock (household), in sound bodily health, with provisions for the day ahead, it is as if they had the whole world in their hands".
(Related by at-Tirmidhī)

Sa‘d ibn Abī Waqqāṣ (*r*) reported that a man came to the Prophet (*ṣ*) and said: “Messenger of Allah, give me some advice, and be brief”. The Prophet (*ṣ*) said: “You must give up hope of having what people possess. Avoid greed: it is ready-made poverty. And avoid anything for which excuses have to be made”.
(Related by al-Ḥākim and al-Bayhaqī)

Ibn ‘Umar (*r*) reported: “The Messenger of Allah (*ṣ*) once grasped me by the shoulder and told me: ‘Be in this world as if you were a stranger or a passer-by’”.

Ibn ‘Umar (*r*) used to say, “When night comes upon you, do not expect [to live to see] the morning; when you wake up in the morning, do not expect [to live to see] the night. Take [benefit] from your [times of] health [in preparation] for [times of] sickness, and from your life for when you are dead.”
(Related by al-Bukhārī)

Chapter 30

Safety from Hell-Fire

Al-Ḥārith ibn Muslim at-Tamīmī (*r*) reported that the Prophet (*ṣ*) told him: "After performing the dawn (*ṣubḥ*) prayer, before you utter another word, say: 'O Allah, save me from Hell-Fire (*Allāhumma ajirnī min an-nār*)' seven times. If you die that day, Allah will decree that you be saved from Hell-Fire. After performing the sunset (*maghrib*) prayer, before you utter another word, say: 'O Allah, save me from Hell-Fire (*Allāhumma ajirnī min an-nār*)' seven times. If you die that night, Allah will decree that you be saved from Hell-Fire."
(Related by an-Nasā'ī and Abū Dā'ūd)

Chapter 31

A man of Paradise

Abū Hurayrah (*r*) reported that an Arab of the desert went to the Prophet (*ṣ*) and said: "O Messenger of Allah, guide me to an action by performing which I may enter Paradise". He replied: "Worship Allah; associate none with Him; keep up the prescribed prayers (*ṣalāt*); pay the obligatory *zakāt*; and fast Ramadan". The man said: "By Him in Whose Hand is my soul, I will do no more and no less than that". When the man turned away [to go], the Prophet (*ṣ*) commented: "Anyone who is gladdened to behold a man from among the people of Paradise should look at this man".
(Related by al-Bukhārī and Muslim)

Chapter 32

Ṣalāt al-Istikhārah (Prayer for Divine Guidance)

Jābir ibn 'Abd Allāh (*r*) said that the Messenger of Allah (*ṣ*) used to teach [the Companions] to ask Divine Guidance (*Istikhārah*) in all matters (*amr*), just as he used to teach them *Sūrah*s of the Qur'ān. He would say: "Whenever any of you are concerned about some matter, let them offer two *rak'ah*s of voluntary prayer, then say: 'O Allah, by Your Knowledge I seek what is best from You, and by Your Omnipotence I ask You for strength, and I ask You of Your Immense Favour (*faḍl*). For You have power while I have not, and You know while I do not: You are the Knower of all things Unseen. O Allah, if You know that this matter is good for me as regards my faith, my life and my final destiny' (or he may have said, 'for my destiny both present and final'), 'then ordain it for me, make it easy for me, and then bless me in it. But if You know that this matter is bad for me as regards my faith, my life and my final destiny' (or he may have said, 'for my destiny both present and final'), 'then keep it away from me and me away from it, and ordain for me that which is best, wherever it may be, and make me content with it'. Then they should mention what they need [guidance about]."

The *du'ā'* in Arabic: *'Allāhumma innī astakhīruka bi-'il-mika wa astaqdiruka bi-qudratika wa as'aluka min faḍlika 'l-'aẓīm, fa-innaka taqdiru wa lā aqdir, wa ta'lamu wa lā a'lam, wa anta 'Allāmu 'l-ghuyūb. Allāhumma in kunta*

ta'lamu anna hādha 'l-amra khayrun lī fī dīnī wa ma'āshī wa 'āqibati amrī fa 'qdurhu lī wa yassirhu lī thumma bārik lī fīh. Wa in kunta ta'lamu anna hādha 'l-amra sharrun lī fī dīnī wa ma'āshī wa 'āqibati amrī fa 'ṣrifhu 'annī wa 'ṣrifnī 'anhu wa 'qdur liya 'l-khayra ḥaythu kāna thumma 'rḍinī bih.'
(Related by al-Bukhārī, Abū Dā'ūd, at-Tirmidhī, an-Nasā'ī, and Ibn Mājah)

On the benefit of *Istikhārah*

Sa'd ibn Abī Waqqāṣ (*r*) reported that the Messenger of Allah (*ṣ*) said: "Part of the happiness of the Son of Adam lies in his praying to Allah Most Mighty and Glorious for guidance".
(Related by Imam Aḥmad ibn Ḥanbal, Abū Ya'lā, and al-Ḥākim)

[One reporter of the *Ḥadīth*] added: "and part of the misery of the Son of Adam lies in his omitting to pray to Allah for guidance".

Chapter 33

A prayer (du'ā') for the relief, by Allah's permission, of anxiety and sorrow

Anas (*r*) reported that the Prophet (*ṣ*) said: "'Alī, shall I teach you a prayer (*du'ā'*) to say to your Lord when you are afflicted by sorrow or anxiety, which He will answer and give you relief, Allah willing? Perform ablution (*wuḍū'*) and offer two *rak'ah*s; then thank Allah and praise Him; invoke blessings on your Prophet; and ask forgiveness for yourself and all Believers, male and female. Then say: 'O Allah, it is You Who judge between Your servants in all their disputes. There is no god but Allah, the Exalted, the Mighty. There is no god but Allah, the Forbearing, the Generous. All Glory to Allah, Lord of the Seven Heavens and Lord of the Mighty Throne. Praise be to Allah, Lord of the Worlds. O Allah, Dispeller of sorrow, Reliever of care, Answerer of the prayer of those who call upon You in their plight; You are the Most Merciful and Compassionate in this world and the Hereafter. Have Mercy on me by fulfilling this need of mine and granting it success, with a mercy that will save me from depending on the mercy of anyone other than You'.

(In Arabic: *'Allāhumma Anta taḥkuma bayna 'ibādika fīmā kānū fīhi yakhtalifūn. Lā ilāha illā 'Llāhu 'l-'Aliyyu 'l-'Aẓīm, la ilāha illā 'Llāhu 'l-Ḥalīmu 'l-Karīm. Subḥāna 'Llāhi Rabbi 's-samāwāti 's-sab'ati wa Rabbi 'l-'Arshi 'l-'Aẓīm. Al-ḥamdu li-'Llāhi Rabbi 'l-'Ālamīn. Allāhumma Kāshifa 'l-ghammi, Mufarrija 'l-hammi, Mujība da'wati 'l-muḍṭarīna idhā dā'ūk, Raḥmāna 'd-dunyā wa 'l-Ākhirati wa Raḥīmahumā, fa-'rḥamnī fī ḥājatī hādhihi bi-qaḍā'ihā wa najāḥihā raḥmatan tughnīnī bika 'an raḥmati man siwāk'.*)
(Related by al-Iṣbahānī)

Ibn 'Abbās (*r*) reported that the Messenger of Allah (*ṣ*)

said: "Gabriel (peace be upon him) brought me some formulae of supplication (*da'awāt*) and said, 'If any worldly affair troubles you, offer these, then ask whatever it is you need: O Originator of the Heavens and Earth, Lord of Majesty and Generosity, You Who are called to by those who cry aloud, Rescuer of those who seek deliverance, Averter of evil, Most Merciful of the merciful, Answerer of the prayers of those under duress, God of the Universe! Unto You I submit this need of mine. You know it best, so ordain it'."

(In Arabic: '*Yā Badī'a 's-samāwāti wa 'l-arḍ, yā Dhā 'l-jalāli wa 'l-ikrām, yā Ṣarīkha 'l-mustaṣrikhīn, yā Ghiyātha 'l-mustaghīthin, yā Kāshifa 's-sū', yā Arḥama 'r-rāḥimīn, yā Mujība da'awāti 'l-muḍṭarīn, yā Ilāha 'l-'ālamīn! Bika anzilu ḥājatī, wa Anta a'lamu bihā fa 'qḍihā.*' (Related by al-Iṣbahānī)

Chapter 34

Prostration in prayer (*sujūd*) leads to Paradise

Abū Firās Rabī'ah ibn Ka'b al-Aslamī (*r*), a servant of the Messenger of Allah (*ṣ*) and one of the People of the Porch (*Ahl aṣ-Ṣuffah*), reported: "When I was staying with Allah's Messenger (*ṣ*), I used to bring him water for ablution and other things he needed. He once said to me, 'Ask me for something!'. I said, 'I ask to be your companion in Paradise'. He asked, 'Anything else?'. I answered, 'Only that'. He said, 'Then help me against your [lower] self by making many prostrations (*sujūd*)'".
(Related by Muslim)

Abū 'Abd ar-Raḥmān Thawbān (*r*), protégé (*mawlā*) of Allah's Messenger (*ṣ*), reported that he heard the Messenger of Allah (*ṣ*) say: "You must prostrate yourself as often as possible: each time you prostrate before Allah, He raises your position in Heaven by one degree and removes one sin from you as reward for it".
(Related by Muslim)

Jābir (*r*) narrated: "I heard the Messenger of Allah (*ṣ*) say: 'There is an hour of the night – every night – when if a Muslim happens to ask something good of Allah, whether it concerns this life or the Next Life, it will be granted him'".
(Related by Muslim)

It is reported on the authority of Abū Mālik al-Ash'arī (*r*) that the Messenger of Allah (*ṣ*) said: "If any man wakes up in the night, awakens his wife – splashing water on her face if sleep overcomes her – and they both arise in their home and invoke Allah (Mighty and Glorious is He) for an hour of the night, Allah will forgive them both".
(Related by aṭ-Ṭabarānī)

According to al-Mughīrah ibn Shu'bah (*r*), the Prophet (*ṣ*) used to stand [in prayer] until his feet became swollen. When people said "[But] Allah has already forgiven all your sins, past and future", he replied: "Then should I not be a thankful servant?".
(Related by al-Bukhārī, Muslim, and an-Nasā'ī)

Ibn 'Abbās (may Allah be pleased with him and his father) said: "The Messenger of Allah (*ṣ*) used to order us to pray at night. To encourage us, he even said, 'Be sure to offer some voluntary night prayers, even if it be only one *rak'ah*'".
(Related by aṭ-Ṭabarānī)

Chapter 35

Feeding people, greeting people, and offering voluntary prayers at night

Abū Hurayrah (*r*) narrated: "I said: 'Messenger of Allah, whenever I see you my soul is comforted and my heart soothed. Tell me about everything'. He replied, 'Everything was created from water'. I said to him, 'Tell me of something to do, by which I may enter Paradise'. He said: 'Feed people; greet people; keep up links with relatives; pray at night while [most] people are asleep. Then you shall enter Paradise'".
(Related by Aḥmad ibn Ḥanbal, Ibn Abī 'd-Dunyā, and Ibn Ḥibbān)

Abū Malik al-Ash'arī (*r*) reported that the Prophet (*ṣ*) said: "There are dwellings in Paradise whose exteriors can be seen from inside, and whose interiors can be seen from outside. Allah has prepared them for those who feed people, greet people, and pray at night while people are asleep".
(Related by Ibn Ḥibbān)

Chapter 36

Generosity towards one's neighbours

Abū Dharr (*r*) reported that the Messenger of Allah (*ṣ*) said: "Abū Dharr, when you make broth add more water, and offer some to your neighbours".
(Related by Muslim)

It is related on the authority of Abū Hurayrah (*r*) that the Messenger of Allah (*ṣ*) said: "Whoever believes in Allah and the Last Day, let him not harm his neighbour. Whoever believes in Allah and the Last Day, let him be generous to his guest. Whoever believes in Allah and the Last Day, let him say that which is good or else be silent".
(Related by al-Bukhārī and Muslim)

Chapter 37

Love the destitute (*al-masākīn*)

Abū Dharr (*r*) said, "My dearest friend [the Prophet] (*ṣ*) advised me to do seven things:

1. To love the destitute, and to be close to them.
2. To think of those worse off than me, not of those better off.
3. To keep up ties with relatives, even if they are harsh with me.
4. To say often, 'There is no power or strength except through Allah (*Lā ḥawla wa lā quwwata illā bi-'Llāh*)'.
5. To tell the truth, however bitter it may be.
6. Not to feel resentment towards Allah when people find fault with me.
7. Never to ask people for anything."

(Related by Aḥmad ibn Ḥanbal and aṭ-Ṭabarānī)

Chapter 38

Definitions of wealth and poverty

Abū Dharr (*r*) reported: "The Messenger of Allah (*ṣ*) said to him: 'Abū Dharr, do you consider that wealth consists in having plenty of property?'. I replied, 'Yes, O Messenger of Allah'. He asked me, 'Do you consider that poverty consists in having little property?'. 'Yes, O Messenger of Allah', I replied. He said: 'The only wealth is wealth in the heart; and the only poverty is poverty in the heart. He who has wealth within his heart cannot be harmed by whatever befalls him in this world. As for him who has poverty within his heart, whatever he may accumulate in this world will never make him rich; all that harms his soul is its greed'."
(Related by Ibn Ḥibbān)

Chapter 39

Fear (*Taqwā*) of Allah, the Mighty, the Glorious

Abū Dharr (*r*) related: "I once asked, 'O Messenger of Allah, give me some advice'. He replied, 'You must fear Allah, for that is the heart of the matter'. I said, 'O Messenger of Allah, tell me more'. He answered, 'You must recite the Qur'ān, for it is a Light for you on Earth, and a Treasure for you in Heaven'".
(From a lengthy *Ḥadīth* related by Ibn Ḥibbān)

'Abd Allāh ibn 'Amr ibn al-'Āṣ (*r*) reported: "The Messenger of Allah (*ṣ*) said: 'One who habitually reads the Qur'ān will be told [in the next world]: Recite, chant and intone as you used to intone in the lower world; for your spiritual position (*manziluka*) will be found in the last verse that you recite'."
(Related by at-Tirmidhi, Abū Dā'ūd, Ibn Mājah, and Ibn Ḥibbān)

Chapter 40

The excellence of reciting the Qur'ān

Abū Umāmah al-Bāhilī (*r*) reported that he heard the Prophet (*ṣ*) say: "Read the Qur'ān, for on the Day of Resurrection it will come to intercede for those who keep company with it. Read the two Luminous *Sūrah*s, *al-Baqarah* and *Āl 'Imran* [*Sūrah*s II and III)]. On the Day of Resurrection they will come to vouch for those who keep company with them: they will resemble two clouds, or two shading clouds, or two flocks of birds with wings outspread. Recite *Sūrat al-Baqarah*: it is a blessing to take it and a source of regret to leave it, and falsehood (*al-baṭalah*) cannot prevail over it."
(Related by Muslim)

Mu'āwiyah ibn Salām commented: "I have been informed that 'falsehood' here means "those who practise magic (*saḥarah*)."

Chapter 41

Ways of spending in charity

Anas ibn Malik (*r*) reported that a man from [the tribe of] Tamīm went to the Prophet (*ṣ*) and said, "O Messenger of Allah, I have plenty of property, a family, and ready cash. Tell me, how should I act: How should I give in charity?". The Messenger of Allah (*ṣ*) replied: 'Pay the *zakāh* on your wealth: that will purify your wealth. Maintain good relations with your relatives. Recognize the rights of the poor, of neighbours, and of beggars'."
(Related by Aḥmad ibn Ḥanbal)

Chapter 42

A prayer to ease trouble and for the discharge of debts, by permission of Allah, the Exalted

According to Abū Sa'īd al-Khudrī (*r*), Allah's Messenger (*ṣ*) once went into the Mosque and found a man of the Anṣār called Abū Umāmah sitting there. He [ṣ] said to the man, 'Abū Umāmah, how is it that I see you sitting in the Mosque when it is not prayer-time?'. He replied, "Some worries and debts are troubling me, O Messenger of Allah". [The Prophet (*ṣ*)] said, "Shall I teach you something to say, that Allah Most Mighty and Glorious may relieve you of worries and pay off your debts?". He answered, "Yes indeed, O Messenger of Allah".

[The Prophet (*ṣ*)] told him, "Every morning and evening, say: 'I seek refuge with You [Allah] from worry and from sadness. I seek refuge with You from weakness and from sloth. I seek refuge with You from meanness and cowardice. I seek refuge with You from being overcome by debt and from being subjugated by men'". [Abū Sa'īd (*r*) continued]: "I did so, and then Allah Most Mighty and Glorious took away my worries and paid my debts".

(The prayer in Arabic: '*Allāhumma innī a'ūdhu bika mina 'l-hammi wa 'l-ḥazan, wa a'ūdhu bika mina 'l-'ajzi wa 'l-kasal, wa a'ūdhu bika mina 'l-bukhli wa 'l-jubn, wa a'ūdhu bika min ghalabati 'd-dayni wa qahri 'r-rijāl.*') (Related by Abū Dā'ūd)

Chapter 43

A prayer to say before going to sleep

Abū 'Umārah al-Barrā' ibn 'Āzib (*r*) reported that the Messenger of Allah (*ṣ*) said: "When you go to bed, say: 'O Allah, I submit my soul to You; I turn my face towards You; I entrust all my affairs to You; I rely upon You for support and protection, in hope of You and in fear of You. There is no refuge or safety but with You. I believe in the Book You revealed, and in the Prophet You sent (*Allāhumma aslamtu nafsī ilayk, wa wajahtu wajhī ilayk, wa alja'tu ẓahrī ilayk, raghbatan wa rahbatan ilayk. Lā maljā'a wa lā manjā'a minka illā ilayk. Āmantu bi-Kitabika 'lladhī anzalta wa bi-Nabiyyika 'lladhī arsalt*)'. If you die that night, you will die in the *Fiṭrah* (the state of natural purity and guidance); and if you live to see the next dawn, you will find goodness (*khayr*)."
(Related by al-Bukhārī and Muslim)

According to Abū Sa'īd al-Khudrī (*r*), the Prophet (*ṣ*) said: "He who says, when he goes to bed, 'I ask forgiveness of Allah, than Whom there is no other god, the Living, the Self-Sustaining; and I repent unto Him (*Astaghfiru 'Llāha 'lladhī lā ilāha illā Huwa 'l-Ḥayya 'l-Qayyūma wa atūba ilayh*)', Allah will forgive all his sins, be they as much as the sea's foam, the leaves on the trees, the desert sands, or the days of the Universe's being".
(Related by at-Tirmidhī)

It is reported on the authority of Anas ibn Mālik (*r*) that the Messenger of Allah (*ṣ*) said: "He who says, when he goes to bed, 'Praise be to Allah, Who has fulfilled my needs and granted me shelter. Praise be to Allah, Who has provided me with food and drink. Praise be to Allah, Who has bestowed abundant blessings upon me (*al-Ḥamdu li-'Llāhi 'lladhī kafānī wa āwānī. Al-ḥamdu li-'Llāhi 'lladhī aṭ'amanī wa saqānī. Al-ḥamdu li-'Llāhi 'lladhī manna 'alayya fa-afḍal*)' praises Allah with the equivalent of the praises of all creation combined."
(Related by al-Bayhaqī)

Chapter 44

A prayer for those afflicted with insomnia at night

Zayd ibn Thābit (*r*) narrated as follows: "I complained to the Messenger of Allah (*ṣ*) that I was suffering from insomnia. He told me, 'Say, O Allah, the stars have faded away and eyes have rested in sleep, but You are the Ever-Living, the Self-Sustaining. Neither tiredness nor sleep overtake You. O Ever-Living, Self-Sustaining One, make my night quiet and close my eyes in slumber'. (In Arabic: '*Allāhumma ghārati 'n-nujūm, wa hādati 'l-'uyūn, wa Anta Ḥayyun Qayyūm. Lā ta'khudhuka sinatun wa lā nawm. Yā Ḥayyu yā Qayyūmu ahdi' laylī wa anim 'aynī*)'. I spoke those words and Allah Most Mighty and Glorious cured me of the malady I had suffered."
(Related by Ibn as-Sunnī)

Allah's Messenger (*ṣ*) taught Khālid ibn al-Walīd (*r*) the following when he suffered insomnia: "O Allah, Lord of the Seven Heavens and all that they shelter, Lord of the Worlds and all that they sustain, Lord of the Shayṭāns and of all whom they mislead! Be my Refuge against the evil of every one of Your creatures, that none of them may transgress against me or oppress me. Mighty is Your Refuge, and glorious is Your praise". In Arabic: "*Allāhumma Rabba 's-samāwāti 's-sab'i wa mā aẓallat, wa Rabba 'l-arḍīna wa mā aqallat, wa Rabba 'sh-shayāṭīna wa mā aḍallat, kun lī jāran min sharri khalqika kullihim jamī'an an yafruṭa 'alayya aḥadun minhum aw an yaṭghà; 'azza jāruka wa jalla thanā'uk*".
(Related by at-Tirmidhī and aṭ-Ṭabarānī)

Chapter 45

The Best of People

Abū Sa'īd al-Khudrī (*r*) narrated that man once asked: "O Messenger of Allah, who is the best of people?". He replied: "A Believer who strives in the Way of Allah with his self and his property". The man then asked: "Who is the next best?". He [*ṣ*] replied: "A man who lives in isolation among some nation of people, devoting himself to the worship of his Lord".
(Related by al-Bukhārī and Muslim)

It is also reported on the authority of Abū Sa'īd al-Khudrī that the Messenger of Allah (*ṣ*) once said: "The time will come when the best property that a Muslim may have is a flock of sheep with which he follows the mountaintops and places where the rain falls, fleeing to save his Faith from calamitous trials (*fitan*)".
(Related by al-Bukhārī)

Chapter 46

Making amends (*kaffārah*) after sitting in a gathering

Abū Hurayrah (*r*) reported that the Messenger of Allah (*ṣ*) said: "Anyone who sits in a gathering wherein there has been a great deal of clamour, and says before rising to leave: 'Glory be to You, O Allah, Praise be to You. I bear witness that there is no god but You. I seek Your forgiveness and turn to You in repentance (*Subḥānaka 'Llāhumma wa bi-ḥamdik, ashhadu an lā ilāha illā anta. Astaghfiruka wa atūba ilayk*)', will be forgiven the wrongs that they committed in that gathering".
(Related by Abū Dā'ūd, at-Tirmidhī, an-Nasā'ī, Ibn Ḥibbān, and al-Ḥākim)

Chapter 47

The merit of glorifying Allah *(Tasbīḥ)*

Abū Dharr (*r*) reported that Allah's Messenger (*ṣ*) once asked him, "Shall I tell you the words most loved by Allah?". Abū Dharr (*r*) replied, "Messenger of Allah, do tell me the words most loved by Allah". He told me, "The words most loved by Allah are: 'Glory be to Allah, and all Praise to Him (*Subḥāna 'Llāhi wa bi-ḥamdih*)'".
(Related by Muslim and an-Nasā'ī)

Muslim transmitted a similar *Ḥadīth*, in which the Prophet (*ṣ*) was asked "Which words are best?", to which he replied: "Those which Allah chose for His angels and for His servants: 'Glory be to Allah, and all Praise to Him (*Subḥāna 'Llāhi wa bi-ḥamdih*)'".

'Abd Allāh ibn 'Amr (*r*) reported that the Messenger of Allah (*ṣ*) said, "He who says 'Glory be to Allah, and all Praise to Him (*Subḥāna 'Llāhi wa bi-ḥamdih*)' will have a palm tree planted for him in Paradise".

Abū Hurayrah (*r*) reported that the Messenger of Allah (*ṣ*) said: "Two phrases which are light on the tongue, weighty in the Scales [of Judgement], and beloved of the All-Merciful: 'Glory be to Allah, and all Praise to Him (*Subḥāna 'Llāhi wa bi-ḥamdih*)', and 'Glory to Allah, the Mighty (*Subḥāna 'Llāhi 'l-'Aẓīm*)'".
(Related by al-Bukhārī, Muslim, and at-Tirmidhī)

Chapter 48

The "master prayer" for forgiveness (*sayyidu 'l-istighfār*)

According to Shaddād ibn 'Aws (*r*), the Prophet (*ṣ*): "The 'master prayer' for forgiveness of Allah is to say, 'O Allah, You are my Lord; there is no god but You. You created me and I am Your servant. I am keeping my pledge and promise to you as best I can. I seek refuge with You from any evil I have done. I acknowledge the blessings You have given me, and I confess my sins to You, so forgive me; for truly none can forgive sins but You'. Those who say this *du'ā* in the daytime, with sure faith (*mūqinan*) in it, and then die that same day, are destined for Paradise. Those who say this *du'ā'* at night, with sure faith in what they say, and then die that same night, are destined for Paradise".

The prayer in Arabic: *'Allāhumma Anta Rabbī. Lā ilāha illā Ant. Khalaqtanī wa anā 'abduk. Wa anā 'alà 'ahdika wa wa'dika ma 'staṭa't. A'ūdhu bika min sharr mā ṣana't. Abū'u laka bi-ni'matika 'alayya wa abū'u bi-dhanbī. Fa-'ghfir lī fa-innahu lā yaghfiru 'dh-dhunūba illā Ant'.* (Related by al-Bukhārī)

Chapter 49

Plants of Paradise

Abū Hurayrah (*r*) reported: "The Prophet (*ṣ*) once came past me as I was planting a plant and asked, 'What is it that you are planting, Abū Hurayrah?' 'Some plants', I replied. He said, 'Shall I guide you to plants which are better than this? Say: Glory to Allah, and praise to Allah! There is no god but Allah, and Allah is Most Great (*Subḥāna 'Llāhi wa 'l-ḥamdu li-'Llāhi wa lā ilāha illa 'Llāhu wa 'Llāhu Akbar*). For each of these [phrases] a tree will be planted for you in Paradise'."
(Related by Ibn Mājah and al-Ḥākim)

Chapter 50

Protection (*ta'wīdhah*) against scorpion stings

Abū Hurayrah (*r*) narrated that a man went to the Prophet (*ṣ*) and told him, "Messenger of Allah, yesterday I came across a scorpion and it stung me". He replied: "If only you had said last night, 'I seek refuge with the Perfect Words of Allah from the evil of what He created (*A'ūdhu bi-kalimāti 'Llāhi 't-tāmmāti min sharri mā khalaq*)', it would not have harmed you".
(Related by Mālik, Muslim, and at-Tirmidhī)

According to another version of the *Ḥadīth*, the Prophet (*ṣ*) said, "Whoever says three times at night, 'I seek refuge with the Perfect Words of Allah from the evil of what He created (*A'ūdhu bi-kalimāti 'Llāhi 't-tāmmāti min sharri mā khalaq*)' will not be harmed by [the scorpion's] venom that night".

Suhayl added: "So our people used to learn this prayer and recite it every night. Then one day a slave girl was bitten, but she felt no pain from it."

[There is a saying:] "[Recite] 'the Mother of the Book' [*al-Fātiḥah*] as a spell over those who have been bitten."

Abū Sa'īd al-Khudrī (*r*) narrated the following incident. Some Companions of Allah's Messenger (*ṣ*) went on a journey. While travelling they stopped among a community of desert Arabs. The Companions asked them for hospitality, but they refused to give it. The leader of that Community was then bitten by some poisonous insect. His people tried everything, but nothing they did helped him. They said to one another, "Why don't we go to those people who stopped here in case they have something?".

So they went to [the Companions] and told them, "You people, our leader has received a [poisonous] bite. We have tried everything to help him but it has done him no good. Has any of you anything [that might help?]". One of the Companions said, "By Allah, truly I can cast a spell [to cure him] – but by Allah, we asked you for hospitality but you would not give it. So I will not cast the spell [for him] until you give us some reward." They then agreed upon a number of sheep [as reward].

The Companion then went off to [the sick man]: he spat upon him and recited "All praise to Allah, Lord of the Universe" [i.e. *al-Fātiḥah*]. [The reaction was] as though the man was set free from shackles: he began walking about and there was nothing wrong with him. Thereupon [the desert Arabs] paid the agreed reward to [the Companions], and some of them said, "Distribute it". The man who had cast the curative spell said, "Do not do so until we reach the Prophet (ṣ) and mention to him what happened; then we shall see what he orders us to do".

In due course they came before the Prophet (ṣ) and told him of the incident. He asked: "But how did you know that [*al-Fātiḥah*] was a curative spell?". Then he observed, "You hit the mark. Divide up [your reward] and give me a share in it along with you". Then the Prophet (ṣ) smiled.

(This, the fullest version of the *Ḥadīth*, is related by al-Bukhārī)

Chapter 51

A prayer for the discharging of one's debts and for abundant provision, by the permission of Allah

It is reported on the authority of 'Ā'ishah (*r*) that [her father] Abū Bakr aṣ-Ṣiddīq (*r*) came to her once and told her: "I have heard from the Messenger of Allah (*ṣ*) a prayer (*du'ā'*) which he has taught me". "What is it?", she asked. [Abū Bakr] told her: "Jesus the son of Mary used to teach his disciples the following: 'If any of you had debts like a mountain of gold and called upon Allah with this *du'ā'*, Allah would repay it for him'. [The prayer is:] O Allah, Reliever from worries, Answerer of the supplications of those in distress, the All-Merciful and Most Compassionate in this world and the Hereafter! You have mercy on me, so have such mercy on me that I have no need of compassion from anyone but You'". Abū Bakr said, "I therefore used to make this supplication to Allah, and Allah brought me such a profit that my debt was paid off".

(The prayer in Arabic: '*Allāhumma Fārija 'l-hammi, Kāshifa 'l-ghammi, Mujība da'wati 'l-muḍṭarrīn, Raḥmāna 'd-dunyā wa 'l-ākhirati wa Raḥīmahumā. Anta tarḥamunī fa 'rḥamnī bi-raḥmatin tughnīnī bihā 'an raḥmati man siwāk.*')

'Ā'ishah (*r*) also related as follows: "I used to make the same supplication; and I had not long to wait before Allah gave me provision – and not in the form of charity or bequests. Allah paid off my debt: I distributed a good share among my relatives; set free the daughter of 'Abd ar-Raḥmān for three okkas of gold leaf; and there was still a good deal left over for us."
(Reported by al-Bazzār, al-Ḥākim, and al-Iṣbahānī)

It is reported on the authority of Mu'ādh ibn Jabal that the Prophet (ṣ) said: "Mu'ādh, should I not teach you a prayer? Even if you were faced with a debt as heavy as [Mount] Ṣibīr [in Yemen] Allah would discharge it for you if you used this supplication. Mu'ādh, pray like this: 'Say, O Allah, Master of all Dominion! You bestow kingship on whom You will, and You take kingship from whom You will. All good is in Your Hand. You are Powerful over all things. You bring night into day, and You bring day into night. You bring forth the living from the dead, and You bring forth the dead from the living. You provide for whomever You will beyond all measure. [Qur'ān: III, 26-27].' 'All-Merciful One of this world and the Hereafter! You give of them to Whom You will and withhold from whom You will. Have such mercy on me that I have no need of compassion from anyone but You'".

(The prayer in Arabic: *'Quli 'Llāhumma Mālika 'l-Mulki tu'tī 'l-mulka man tashā'u wa tanzi'u 'l-mulka mimman tashā'u wa tu'izzu man tashā'u wa tudhillu man tashā'. Bi-yadika 'l-khayru innaka 'alā kulli shay'in Qadīr. Tūliju 'l-layla fī 'n-nahāri wa tūliju 'n-nahāra fī 'l-layli wa tukhriju 'l-ḥayya mina 'l-mayyiti wa tukhriju 'l-mayyita mina 'l-ḥayy. Wa tarzuqu man tashā'u bi-ghayri ḥisāb.' 'Raḥmāna 'd-dunyā wa 'l-ākhirati wa Raḥīmahumā tu'ṭī man tashā'u minhā wa tamna'u man tashā'. Irḥamnī raḥmatan tughnīnī bi-hā 'an raḥmati man siwāk.*)
(Related by aṭ-Ṭabarānī)

Chapter 52

Spending in different forms of charity

'Abd Allāh ibn 'Amr ibn al-'Āṣ (*r*) reported that a man once asked the Messenger of Allah (*ṣ*): "What is the best thing in Islam?". He replied: "That you offer food in charity, and give greetings to those whom you know as well as those whom you do not know".
(Related by al-Bukhārī and Muslim)

Abū Hurayrah (*r*) reported that the Messenger of Allah (*ṣ*) said: "No day dawns upon [Allah's] servants without two angels descending [to Earth]. One of them says, 'O Allah, give recompense (*khalaf*) to those who give [charity]!'; the other says, 'O Allah, give loss (*talaf*) to those who withhold [charity]!'.
(Related by al-Bukhārī and Muslim)

According to Ibn Mas'ūd (*r*), the Prophet (*ṣ*) said: "There are only two kinds of people whom one may envy: a man to whom Allah granted wealth and the power to use it all rightly [i.e. charitably]; and a man to whom Allah granted wisdom and who used it in judgement and taught it to others".
(Related by al-Bukhārī and Muslim)

Ibn Mas'ūd (*r*) also reported that Allah's Messenger (*ṣ*) said: "Who amongst you loves his heirs' wealth more than his own?". The answer was: "O Messenger of Allah, we all love our own wealth best". [The Prophet (*ṣ*)] explained: "A person's own wealth is what he has sent ahead [for reward in the Hereafter, by giving charity etc.]; and his heirs' wealth is what he leaves behind".
(Related by al-Bukhārī)

'Adī ibn Ḥātim (*r*) reported that the Messenger of Allah (*ṣ*) said: "Keep away from Hell-Fire, even if only giving away in charity a piece of dried date".
(Related by al-Bukhārī and Muslim)

Abū Hurayrah (*r*) narrated that the Messenger of Allah (*ṣ*) said: "Allah Most High has said, 'Spend to provide for people, O son of Adam, and you will be provided for'." (Related by al-Bukhārī and Muslim)

Chapter 53

Prayers (*du'ā's*) to say in the morning, at night, and when leaving one's house

Abū Hurayrah (*r*) reported that Abū Bakr aṣ-Ṣiddīq (*r*) asked: "O Messenger of Allah, command me to recite some words in the morning and at night". [The Prophet (*ṣ*)] told him: "Say: 'O Allah, Creator of the Heavens and the earth, Knower of all things; Lord and owner of all things! I bear witness that there is no god but You. I seek refuge with You from the evil of my own soul and from the evil and the idolatry (*shirk*) of Satan'. Say this is the morning and in the evening, and when you lie down to sleep."

(The prayer in Arabic: "*Allāhumma Fāṭira 's-samāwāti wa 'l-arḍ, 'Ālima 'l-ghaybi wa 'sh-shahādah, Rabba kulli shay'in wa Malīkah; Ashhadu an lā ilāha illā Ant. A'ūdhu bika min sharri nafsī wa min sharri 'sh-Shayṭāni wa shirkih.*)

(Related by Abū Dā'ūd and at-Tirmidhī)

The Mother of the Believers Umm Salamah (*r*) reported that the Prophet (*ṣ*) used to say this *du'ā'* whenever he left his house: "In the Name of Allah, I put my trust in Allah. O Allah, I seek refuge with You lest I mislead or be misled; lest I make a mistake or be affected by one; lest I commit a wrong or suffer one; and lest I commit foolish behaviour or suffer it'."

(The prayer in Arabic: "*Bi 'smi 'Llāhi tawakkaltu 'alà 'Llāh. Allāhumma innī a'ūdhu bika an aḍilla aw uḍill, aw azilla aw uzall, aw aẓlima aw uẓlam, aw ajhala aw yujhala 'alayy*".)

(Related by Abū Dā'ūd and at-Tirmidhī)

It is reported by Anas (*r*) that the Prophet (*ṣ*) said: "Anyone who utters these words as he comes out from his

home: 'In the Name of Allah, I put my trust in Allah; there is no power or strength except through Allah (*Bi 'smi 'Llāhi, tawakkaltu 'ala 'Llāh, wa lā ḥawla wa lā quwwata illā bi-'Llāh*)' is told: 'You will be guided and guarded, and your needs will be met'; and Satan is kept away from him."
(Related by Abū Dā'ūd and at-Tirmidhī)

Anas ibn Mālik (*r*) reported that the Prophet (*ṣ*) said to Faṭimah (*r*), "What prevents you from listening to the advice that I give you? Say this every morning and every night: 'O Ever-Living, Self-Sustaining One, I seek help through Your Mercy. Set all my affairs to rights, and let me not rely on myself, even for the twinkling of an eye (*Yā Ḥayyu, yā Qayyūmu, bi-raḥmatika astaghīth. Aṣliḥ lī sha'nī kullah, wa lā takilnī ilā nafsī ṭarfata 'ayn*)'."
(Related by an-Nasā'ī and al-Bazzār)

Chapter 54

Do not ask to be made a leader

Abū Sa'īd 'Abd ar-Raḥmān ibn Samūrah (*r*) reported that the Messenger of Allah (*ṣ*) told him: "O 'Abd ar-Raḥman ibn Samūrah, do not ask for leadership. If it is given to you unasked for, you will be supported in it. But if you obtain it at your own request, you will be entrusted with the entire responsibility. Also, if you make a covenant but then find a better one, do that which is better, and do penance (*kaffārah*) for your [broken] covenant".
(Related by al-Bukhārī and Muslim)

Abū Dharr (*r*) reported: "I once asked, 'Messenger of Allah, will you not appoint me as a leader?" [The Prophet (*ṣ*)] struck my shoulder with his hand and replied: "Abū Dharr, you are weak and [leadership] is a trust (*amānah*). On the Day of Resurrection, it will bring disgrace and remose, except for one who shows himself worthy to take it and fulfils his duties in respect of it".
(Related by al-Bukhārī)

According to Abū Hurayrah (*r*) the Prophet (*ṣ*) said: "You (Muslims) will become eager to assume leadership, and it will be a cause for remorse on the Day of Resurrection".
(Related by al-Bukhārī)

Abū Sa'īd (*r*) and Abū Hurayrah (*r*) reported that the Messenger of Allah (*ṣ*) said: "No Prophet sent by Allah, and no leader (*khalīfah*), is without two groups around him. One group enjoins good and urges him to perform it; the other enjoins evil and urges him to perform it. Those free from error (*ma'ṣūm*) are those whom Allah protects".
(Related by al-Bukhārī)

'Ā'ishah (*r*) reported that the Messenger of Allah (*ṣ*)

said: "If Allah wants goodness for a ruler, He appoints for him a sincere and truthful vizier who reminds him when he forgets [Allah and His Laws], and helps him when he remembers. But if He wishes otherwise, He appoints for him an evil vizier who does not remind him when he forgets and does not help him when he does remember." (Related by Abū Dā'ūd)

Chapter 55

Having a mosque, or prayer room (*masjid*), in the house

'Ā'ishah (*r*) said: "The Messenger of Allah (*ṣ*) commanded us to set up mosques in our houses, and to keep them clean and perfumed.
(Related by Aḥmad ibn Ḥanbal, at-Tirmidhī, and Abū Dā'ūd)

Samrah ibn Jandab (*r*) reported: "The Messenger of Allah (*ṣ*) commanded us to keep [rooms for use as] mosques in our houses; and he ordered us to keep them clean."
(Related by Aḥmad ibn Ḥanbal and at-Tirmidhī)

A concluding message

We conclude this collection of noble instructions with the message of our master the Prophet Abraham, blessings and peace be upon him, to the Community (*Ummah*) of our master the Prophet Muḥammad, Allah's peace and blessings be upon him.

Ibn Mas'ūd (*r*), reported that the Messenger of Allah (*ṣ*) said: "On the night of my Ascension (*Isrā'*) I met the Prophet Abraham, peace be upon him. He said: 'O Muhammad, give my greetings (*salām*) to your Community. Tell them that Paradise has good soil and sweet water; it is level; and that its plants are [the result of their saying]: Glory be to Allah, Praise be to Allah, there is no god but Allah, and Allah is most Great (*Subḥāna 'Llāhi wa 'l-ḥamdu li 'Llāhi wa lā ilāha illā 'Llāhu, wa 'Llāhu Akbar*)'". (Reported by at-Tirmidhī and aṭ-Ṭabarānī)

One version adds: 'and there is no power or strength except by Allah (*wa lā ḥawla wa lā quwwata illā bi 'Llāh*)'.

May Allah bless our master Muḥammad and his family and companions and grant them peace. Peace be upon Allah's Messengers. All Praise is for Allah, Lord of the Universe.

Ten pieces of advice for all Muslims

1. Recite as much of the Qur'ān as you can every day. Ask for peace and blessings of Allah upon His Prophet (ṣ) often.

2. Keep up the five obligatory prayers, as well as voluntary night prayer and the forenoon (ḍuḥā) prayer, even if it be only two *rak'ahs*.

3. Pay your obligatory *zakāt*, and give in charity every day, even if it be only very little. If you cannot afford to, then give it in the form of a kind word. Fast Ramadan, and three days each month.

4. Would you not like to be one of those whom Allah loves? Then love your Prophet Muhammad (ṣ) and his family. Be good to your parents.

5. Would you not like to be one of those who say "O Lord, O Lord" and to whom Allah says "Here I am, O My servant; ask, and it shall be given you"? Your prayers will be answered if you eat only what is good and halal; be just to people, even if it be at your own expense; and show good character in all your dealings with people.

6. Would you not like to be one of those whose supplications are favourably answered, for your written record to be radiant with light on the Day of Resurrection? Purify your heart and repeat frequently "There is no god but Allah (*Lā ilāha illā 'Llāh*)". Ask forgiveness for your sins, and for those of all Believers, male and female. Never let yourself be one of those who forget to call upon Allah.

7. Would you not like to be one of those who give praise and thanks to Allah and are brought near Him? When Allah's servant says "Praise be to Allah", Allah says "My servant has praised and thanked Me"; so be sure to repeat often "Praise be to Allah, and peace be upon His chosen servants (*al-Ḥamdu li-'Llāhi wa salāmun 'alà 'ibādihi 'lladhīna 'ṣṭafà*)".

8. Would you not like to be one of the thankful, and that Allah may make your offspring to be good and pious? Then you should recite the following two verses of thanksgiving:
a. "My Lord, grant that I may be grateful for Your favours, which You have bestowed on me and on my parents, and that I may act righteously so as to please You; and admit me, by Your mercy, to the ranks of Your righteous servants." (*Sūrah* 27, verse 19. In Arabic: "*Rabbi awzi'nī an ashkura ni'mataka 'llatī an'amta 'alayya wa 'alā wālidayya wa an a'mala ṣāliḥan tarḍāhu wa adkhilnī bi-raḥmatika fī 'ibādika ṣ-ṣāliḥīn.*")
b. "O my Lord, grant that I may be grateful for Your favours which You have bestowed on me and upon my parents, and that I may act righteously so as to please You; and make my offspring good for me. I have turned to You in repentance, and I am of those who submit themselves to You (*muslimīm*). (*Sūrah* 46, verse 15. In Arabic: "*Rabbi awzi'nī an ashkura ni'mataka 'llatī an'amta 'alayya wa 'alā wālidayya wa an a'mala ṣāliḥan tarḍāhu wa aṣliḥ lī fī dhurriyyatī. Innī tubtu ilayka wa innī mina 'l-muslimīn.*")

9. Would you not like to be guided as to how to integrate soundly your religious and your worldly affairs? Do your utmost to act according to the Divine Command: "O you who believe, bow down, prostrate yourselves, and adore your Lord; and do good, that you may prosper." (*Sūrah* 22, verse 77).

10. Would you not like to be guided to the heart of the matter? "Say: 'I believe in Allah'; then follow the Straight Path."